When you succeed,
what a joyful sense of satisfaction fills you and those at
your table. I've kissed cooks a thousand times with
gladness for their creations.
They had earned it!

© by Seija Kaarina Cleverley. The book author retains sole copyright to her contributions to this book.

ISBN: 978-0-9961028-0-3

Printed in China

The Blurb-provided layout designs and graphic elements are copyright Blurb Inc. This book was created using the Blurb creative publishing service. The book author retains sole copyright to her contributions to this book.

The Nomad Chef

**Recipes, People, Times, and Places
from a Culinary Odyssey**

by
Seija Kaarina Cleverley

Illustrations by Janina Eppel

My Appreciation

This book is dedicated to my family; my eternal companion Michael and to our precious children, Kristiina, Kaarina, Mikael, and Markus and their spouses Jeff, Derek, Rachel and Katie, to fourteen beloved grandchildren, and to anyone else who can find joy and delight in good food around the dinner table with family and friends.

The Nomad Chef is a project that began to ripen decades ago through collections of recipes from friends and relatives. The very first version was on an old Atari computer over thirty years ago. I had a dream to share these recipes and the stories behind them as an heirloom and a memoir about things which have been meaningful to me. I have tried to follow my aspiration with patience and determination and passion.

This has been possible only with the help of God and many highly prized individuals in my life. My heartfelt appreciation in the latter category goes first to Michael who has given his everything to me from the beginning of our earthly path together. He has always been my best friend, supporter and sweetheart. Michael believed in me and made my book a labor of love during uncountable days and weeks and months managing the computer formatting and design and editing the recipes and stories. Almost all the photographs are his. Our daughters and sons along with their dedicated wives and husbands lent everyday moral support, listening to my unceasing thoughts on my project, and responding with always good suggestions. Their affection for excellent food in their daily lives and through entertaining at their tables is so gratifying to me. A special thanks to our daughter Kaarina who shared her writing talent, going through my manuscripts and providing excellent and helpful ideas on the concept and language. Also special appreciation goes to our son Markus for his help with managing photographs and to our daughter-in-law Rachel for providing important suggestions.

The Nomad Chef exists only because of the generosity of so many talented people. Janina Groenewald Eppel, a longtime friend and exceptionally talented artist bestowed charm and fun to *The Nomad Chef* with her beautiful illustrations. Bill Willison, a cherished friend and gifted graphic artist from London and whose impressive work sits on the walls of Ealing Village Town Hall, provided design and layout suggestions up to the final days of his life.

But at the top of my list, of course, armloads of thanks go to all those who generously shared their recipes with me over the years. Many of them are no longer with us, and I honor their memory by allowing you to share the dishes they cherished and so willingly served me and others. I have chosen to write all the book's stories in the past tense because they remain loving memories to me.

Growing up in Finland made me part of the soil and therefore Finnish nature often lives in my recipes. I hope you will sense that. My table is set! Welcome and enjoy the meal which I have prepared for you.

With deep love and appreciation,

Seija Kaarina Cleverley
Karelia House, Virginia, March 2014
www.thenomadchef.com

With my staff before a garden party at Villa Laura, our Rome residence that looked across the ancient city. Our chef, Simone, on my right, leans on the table. The Ambassador's chef, Ian, is to my left, and to Ian's left, is Luana. You will find recipes from all of us.

Recipes, People, Times, and Places from a Culinary Odyssey

Karen Blixen started her famous book, Out of Africa, with the phrase, "I had a home in Africa." I, too, had a home in Africa, with a staff whose beautiful African children had never been to a supermarket until I took them. I also had homes in London, Rome, Athens, and Helsinki. We had residences in Boston, high in the Rocky Mountains, and Washington, DC. My husband Michael was an American diplomat. Over the years as he rose through the ranks to become Deputy Ambassador and Charge d'Affaires at American Embassies in different international capitals, I had the opportunity to explore and refine one of my happiest hobbies: cooking.

When we joined the American Foreign Service we leaped into a colorful new world. Our first assignment was in Milan, Italy. For someone whose hobby was food and cooking, Italy, with its culinary splendor and refined people, was at once both exhilarating and intimidating. It is one thing to enjoy cooking and good food on a personal level, but quite another to be faced with the expectation of hosting refined, sophisticated dinners that have a professional purpose. But my odyssey was under way.

Over the years, I served at my table four-star generals, archbishops, movie stars, university presidents, ambassadors, congressmen, parliamentarians, trade union bosses, and business executives, not to mention a growing family and many friends who visited us in the exotic places where we lived. I eventually employed professional chefs, but for many years, I was the cook, baker, and chef. As I learned and grew, it empowered me with pleasure and confidence especially since it all centered around one of my favorite places, my kitchen.

It was an odyssey where one success bred another, all culminating in wonderful moments around the table with family and guests happily sharing their thoughts and experiences as we feasted upon my creations. Above all, I learned the simplicity of great food and shared the human universals inherent in culinary tradition and rituals. Personal and cultural identity and heritage are deeply tied to our food and dishes.

In *The Nomad Chef* I share some of the most exquisite recipes that I gathered on the culinary journey I traveled for over 30 years. From Idaho to Cameroon, from Italy to South Africa, I collected recipes from many kitchens, from professionals such as Peter in Athens, perhaps the best chef I encountered anywhere, to wonderful cooks, bakers, and chefs from all walks of life, such as Kaija in Finland, who from a penniless young teenager living on her own meager means, became a home economics teacher and and an extraordinarily gifted cook and baker.

But, I am not sharing with you a collection of recipes only. The Nomad Chef is equally a chronicle, telling the stories of those who prepared for us these marvelous dishes and the settings where we served or were served them. Just like good cooking should always be, my recipes are fun, light, and entertaining. Warmth, thought and love have gone into each of them and their stories.

Please join my nomadic adventures to sample some of the finest dishes you can find anywhere, to meet the unforgettable cooks and friends with whom I bonded, and to learn of the rich culinary traditions behind them.

The Nomad Chef is more than just a collection of recipes. It is a record and tribute to those who have woven their colorful stories as threads into my fabric. These are recipes from real people, enjoying real food, in real places.

As I approached people and explained my project, or slipped into the kitchens of gourmet restaurants to learn about their dishes, I found people gladly shared their recipes, and my recipe collection began to grow. I also worked with my staffs to develop dishes that took advantage of the fragrant tastes and rich traditions of the countries where I lived.

Many of my recipes come from what I call the folk kitchen, meals prepared from family recipes passed from generation to generation. There are lasting reasons why recipes are handed down, and thankfully, the folk kitchen still has a place in today's fast-food world. It still exists everywhere. Wonderful home dishes are not rare. I have enjoyed meals from the family kitchen of an Italian truck-driver and his wife that surpassed in their simplicity and refinement many that we ate at some of Italy's finest restaurants. In *The Nomad Chef* you will find folk recipes for breads, cakes, and pastries that a commercial bakery would only hope to have. Long live the culinary legacy and traditions of our ancestors!

I love to cook.

It is not only my hobby, but my identity and purpose. It is my life. But when I prepare meals, I think of those people for whom I cook, and I think of those who have cooked for me. Ultimately, cooking is about people. People were the fascinating part of my culinary journeys, adding meaningful life, spirit and unforgettable flavor to everywhere we lived and visited. These recipes are the timeless remains of those days.

I find many people are intimidated when it comes to entertaining. But ultimately making good food is something anyone can learn to do. From my folk kitchen recipes as well as from those of professional chefs, I learned that some of the biggest hits were dishes that could be served one day to an ambassador and on another to your children, relatives, or friends.

And when you succeed, what a joyful sense of satisfaction fills you and those at your table. I've kissed cooks a thousand times with joy for their creations. They had earned it!

I come from a tradition of baking, cooking, parties, and good friends. My mother and grandparents fled the Russian armies at the end of World War II with little more than the clothes they wore. Father joined us later when he was released from a Russian POW camp. We always enjoyed company, and even a simple meal was prepared with care and love.

My parents and grandparents had lost everything, but no matter how impoverished, they still treasured each moment with friends and made every meal a feast.

Recipes and Page Numbers

Starters and Appetizers

Cheese Pies *15*
Greek Shrimp *17*
Kalamarakia Tiganita *19*
Orange and Olive Appetizer *22*
Parma Ham and Grissini *24*
Samosas *26*
Spinach Pies *29*
Strawberry Salsa *31*
Trout Mousse *33*

First Courses and Pastas

Asparagus in White Sauce *36*
Chickpea Polenta *39*
Lasagna with Radicchio *42*
Lasagna Romana *44*
Pasta Sauce - Red with Sausage *47*
Pasta Sauce - Tomato and Basil *51*
Pasta Sauce - White *55*
Pasta al Mare *56*
Risotto con Erbe *58*
Risotto Milanese *60*
Seafood Spaghetti *63*

Main Courses

Beef Tenderloin al Barolo *68*
Bobotie *70*
Cameroonian Fish with Tomato *74*
Chicken with Lemon and Oil *77*
Chicken with Rosmary *80*
Cottolette *82*
Finnish Holiday Ham *84*
Fried Chicken *87*
Greek Lemon Chicken *91*
Pork Chops in Mustard *94*
Roast Loin of Pork and Prunes *96*
Salmon Baked in Cream *98*
Tenderloin Fillet *100*
Turkey Roast with Orange Sauce *102*
Vitello Tonnato *105*

Soups and Salads

Carrot Soup *108*
Crab Salad *111*
Cream of Apple Soup *114*
Eggplant Salad *117*
Esau's Red Lentil Soup *121*
Insalata Romana *123*
Mediterranean Soup *125*
Parmesan Cheese Boats *128*
Pasta Salad *131*
Reindeer Salad with Grapefruit *133*
Tuna Salad *136*

Vegetables and Rice

Croquette Potatoes *140*
Egyptian Rice *142*
French Baby Peas *144*
Italian Baked Tomatoes *147*
Mykonian Stuffed Tomatoes *149*
Red Lentil Curry *152*
Savory Potatoes *154*
Sri Lankan Rice *156*

Breads and Pastries

Beebop-a-reebop Rhubarb Pie *160*
Chocolate Brownies *162*
Chocolate Chip Cookies *164*
Chocolate Roll Cookies *166*
Christmas Tarts *168*
Coconut Cookies *171*
Cowboy Cookies *173*
Finnish Cinnamon Rolls and Pulla *175*
Graham Rolls *180*
Holiday Stollen *182*
Idaho Potato Doughnuts *186*
Oven Pancake *188*
Pumpernickel Bread *190*
Walnut Bread *192*

Sweets, Cakes, and Desserts

American Chocolate Cake *196*
Baklava *198*
Buttermilk Cake *200*
Chocolate Mousse Pie *202*
Date Cake *204*
Finnish Cream Cake *206*
Frozen Berry Dessert *209*
Genoise Gateau *212*
Mamsel's Torta *216*
Oatmeal Cake *220*
Pavlova *225*
Profiteroles *227*
Perfect Chocolate Sauce *230*
Rhubarb & Strawberry Soup *232*
Supreme au Chocolat *234*
Whipped Cranberry Pudding *237*

English - Metric Conversions

Although I use English measurements in my recipes, I know many of my readers may use metric measurements in their kitchens. These charts will help you make quick conversions.

Volume

1/4 tsp (teaspoon)	=	1.0 ml
1/2 tsp	=	2.5 ml
1 tsp	=	5.0 ml
1 Tb (tablespoon)	=	15.0 ml
2 Tbs	=	30.0 ml
1/4 cup	=	59.0 ml
1/2 cup	=	118.0 ml
1 cup	=	237.0 ml
4 cups	=	.95 l
1 qt (quart)	=	.95 l
1 gal (gallon)	=	3.80 l

Temperature

Fahrenheit		Centigrade
32	=	0
200	=	93
250	=	121
300	=	149
350	=	177
400	=	204
450	=	232
500	=	260

Weight

1/4 oz (ounce)	=	7 g
1 oz	=	28 g
5 oz	=	142 g
8 oz	=	227 g
16 oz	=	454 g
1 lb (pound)	=	454 g
2.2 lbs	=	1 kg

Starters and Appetizers

Cheese Pies *("Tiropites")*
from Cadio's kitchen, Greece

Servings: 12-16

This "tiropita" is from my wonderful Greek friend, Cadio. She served it to us one summer evening in her beautiful Athens residence as an opener to a tasteful meal. Cheese Pies are a mainstay dish in Greece, often placed alongside spinach pies at both restaurants and at home dinner parties. I have many recipes for cheese pies, but this one is one of the very best I had in Greece.

Cadio

- ½ of a 16 oz package of Fillo Dough Pastry
- 8 oz Feta Cheese, grated
- 8 oz Gruyere Cheese, grated
- 8 oz Parmesan Cheese (or other hard Italian cheese), grated
- 4 Eggs, beaten
- 1 cup Cream
- Some Sesame Seeds

Beat the eggs and then mix with the cheeses. Add the cream and pepper.

Prepare your pastry by first dividing ½ package of fillo dough into two portions and cover one portion with a moist towel. Oil a Pyrex dish and add one Fillo sheet at a time, brushing each with melted butter, until you have lined the dish with one of the two portions from the fillo package. Next, cover these sheets with the cheese mixture and layer in the same way the second portion, one sheet at a time, brushing each with melted butter as you go. Brush the top of the dough with melted butter and sprinkle with some sesame seeds. Cut the raw pie into two-inch square slices before baking. Cook in the oven at 400 F for about 25 - 30 minutes.

You may also use Puff Pastry to make small individual pies that are baked on a cookie sheet.

Instead of Fillo pastry you may use home-made pastry dough.

"Calhoun House"

On my culinary odyssey I found life was always full of fun, surprises, and coincidence. This recipe emanated from just one such moment when paths unexpectedly crossed. That is how we met Cadio and her husband, Takis.

It happened at a wedding in Athens where we were seated next to them. During our conversation we found that they owned in downtown Athens a large department store where we had often shopped. As our dinner chat progressed, we were surprised to learn that Takis's grandfather had built the residence where we lived, the "Calhoun House" as the American Embassy called it. The Embassy purchased the Calhoun House during the late 1940's. It was a protected building with a historical past. During World War II, some said, the Greek Resistance met in the basement. Another story claimed that the Nazi occupiers used it as a headquarters.

Takis told us that he and his many cousins had moved to the home for part of the war years. Its large garden produced food for the families during those bad times when the Nazi occupation led many in Athens to starvation. After the war, he added, the Orthodox Archbishop had purchased the residence, but only lived there for a short period.

From our side, we recounted an event when fourteen guests were invited to the home for a sit-down dinner. One of the guests regretted at the last minute, and the dinner table ended up with thirteen, an unlucky number in Greece like in many countries. A few days later, news arrived that one of the guests had suddenly passed away. Someone present that evening remembered the table with thirteen, and a few days later an Orthodox priest arrived at the residence unannounced. He blessed the house to make it fit again for good fortune - and many future dinner parties.

Greek Shrimp Appetizer

Servings 4

from Martha's kitchen, Virginia

This is an easy recipe for a succulent shrimp starter. It is a delightful appetizer, or it can be part of a buffet-style table along with almost any kind of other dishes. Don't hesitate, go ahead and try Martha's shrimp as an opener to one of your meals! As a Greek proverb goes: "The beginning is half of every action."

Martha and her husband Paul

- 1 lb Shrimp with tails
- 3 Tbs Olive Oil
- 3 Tbs Butter, melted (or clarified butter is even better)
- 5 Garlic Cloves, crushed
- 5 Tbs Italian Parsley, fresh or dried
- 6 pcs Red Pepper Flakes
- ½ tsp Salt
- 2 Lemons, squeezed

Defrost and drain the shrimp very well. In an oven pan, combine the remaining ingredients into a sauce. Then coat the shrimp with the sauce. Let them marinate for half an hour.

Place on a single layer in a casserole dish or other pan, and bake the shrimp in a preheated oven 375 F for about 30 minutes. When the shrimp tails start to curve, they are ready.

Greek Shrimp

Oopaah!

Martha's shrimp recipe brings us again to my beloved Greece! Our entire family knows that Greeks are well known for their generosity and hospitality. Their *filoxenia,* (hospitality or, literally, friendship for strangers) is one the nicest qualities in their fabulously beautiful country. You feel that you are loved and pampered from head to toe.

Martha, my Greek-American neighbor and friend, showed some of her filoxenia by serving this antipasto dish in her home when she had neighborhood ladies over for a book club discussion. I enjoyed her shrimp so much that I immediately wanted the recipe, and here it is.

Although she had never been to Greece, Martha grew up in a Greek-American community with her parents and grandparents. In their homes she mastered excellent Greek and learned many authentic Greek dishes. Her teacher in the kitchen was her "yiayia," or Greek grandmother.

Martha's husband, Paul was a retired Marine officer, and both their sons were military officers. There was a year when life was very stressful for her as one of their sons took a dangerous assignment as a young Army lieutenant in the mountains of Afghanistan. Still, she never lost her fun laugh and humor, nor her pleasure in creating and enjoying good food, such as her shrimp.

Martha and I shared a passion for good food and cooking. As we went tirelessly through food magazines and cookbooks in her well organized and equipped kitchen, we could easily chat about cuisine for hours.

Kalamarakia Tiganita *("Fried Squid")*

Servings: 8

from Gordana's kitchen, Greece

It is sometimes difficult to fry crispy squid that is not soft and a little oil saturated. This enjoyable recipe from Gordana solves that problem.

Gordana and her husband George

2 lbs Squid, fresh or frozen

Salt

Flour

Olive Oil

Lemon slices

If you use frozen squid, it may be tough, so use fresh squid if you can. Soaking the squid in milk for half an hour will help tenderize it.

Clean the squid by peeling off the brown thin skin. Remove the head, ink bag and intestines. Wash well. Slice hoods in ¼ inch rings. Let them dry very well – this is the key for crispy squid. Lay the pieces on paper towels and cover them with another paper towel to soak up the water and moisture. This will take about 10 minutes.

When you see that your squid pieces are dry, sprinkle them lightly with salt and coat them well with flour. Shake off the excess flour and immediately fry your pieces in hot olive oil (in a deep fryer or in a pan with an inch or two of oil) until they take on a beautiful golden color, probably about 2 minutes. Using tongs, set the fried squid again on a clean paper towel-lined plate to catch the extra oil. Serve immediately with plenty of lemons.

Note: You should use the oil only once for frying. If you are preparing a lot of squid you might have to change oil in the middle of frying.

A moonlit evening once spent in Chania

    I received this delightful recipe from Gordana, a young Serbian lawyer who came one summer to Greece and like so many other foreign women found her love in Athens. She was tall, beautiful and exotic, fun, and an excellent cook. We often saw her feeding crowds of friends in their Alepochori summer cottage near Corinth, or on the roof terrace of their Athens home that overlooked the white city during daytime hours and the lights of the Olympic Village in the evening. There was always Greek music, dancing, and eating long into the evening.

    Gordana's husband, George, owned a jewelry store called "Aphrodite" in the ancient Monastiraki district, below the Acropolis. He was one of the most generous men in the world – and it often seemed that he had fed half of the world in neighborhood tavernas or at home. No one paid for George's meal. It was always the other way around.

    Once, when Mike was making an official trip to Crete, we met in Chania where George had another shop. It was our first trip to Chania, and George showed us through the colorful streets of this picturesque historic port and introduced us to some wonderful Cretan delicacies. When we stopped to rest at a coffee shop, Mike excused himself and made his way back to the cashier to pay the bill. She looked over to our table and said, "You are with George, and you want to pay?" She started laughing out loud, turned to a waiter, and said in Greek, "He's with George, and thinks he's going to pay!" The atmosphere was like the taverna scene in the movie *Never on Sunday*. George not only insisted on treating us, but also all the men and women of Mike's security detail, and there were five of them that day.

    We became good friends with George and Gordana and returned their generosity by having them often to our home. One evening I asked George why he always wanted to give so much . He looked at me and replied that he had had a poor childhood, often with little or nothing to eat. His family sometimes survived on food they received through American Marshall Plan assistance during the days after World War II. He had always wanted to pay that back, he said. "Without the Marshall Plan," George expressed, "there wouldn't be a George."

Orange and Olive Appetizer
from Simone's kitchen, Italy

Very simple, but the diverse flavors fit amazingly well together for a fun and unique appetizer. Simone often served it to our guests before everyone sat down to eat.

Simone

Oranges (preferably sweet Blood Oranges)

Green or Kalamata Olives (pitted)

Fennel (fresh)

On a toothpick alternate orange pieces, green (or Kalamata) olives, and fennel (*"finocchio"*).

The flavors of these simple ingredients work so well together that I have often combined them together for a very pleasant salad.

    Simone and I were both Leo's, with the same August 1 birthday. With two "lions" in the kitchen, getting ready for a dinner party was always colorful, but done with fun and good spirit. The name of Simone's grandfather, a victim of the Nazis' atrocities during World War II, has a place of honor on the wall of Rome's Jewish Synagogue along the banks of the Tiber.

    Simone was from Rome and was married to an outstanding American tour guide, Ann, who once took us on the greatest tour of the Vatican we ever had. She introduced us to classical sculptures, important masterpieces of the Renaissance, and to Michelangelo's masterpiece, La Pieta, in St. Peter's Basilica. She made these beauties and sites alive in a way we had never experienced - just like Simone brought rich Italian cuisine unforgettably to life in our kitchen and on our table.

Parma Ham and Grissini

from Aurora's kitchen, Italy

This is a tasty and easy-to-make appetizer for times when you are looking for an appetizers or simply a pleasant mid-day snack along with a nice cooling drink. I have always liked Italian breadsticks, grissini's, for their very thin and crispy texture. They originate in Italy's Piedmont region, and can be served plain or with Parma Ham that has been wrapped around them.

Uncooked Parma Ham, Proscuitto Crudo, is another of my food passions. Its saltiness and intense ham flavor goes well with salads, pasta dishes, sandwiches (panini's), or as an appetizer for an antipasto table. Prosciutto di Parma according to its name comes from the Parma region. It takes over a year to cure.

Si mangia bene ("One eats well") in Italy ...and often effortlessly.

Aurora and her husband Giovanni

Parma Ham (or similar prosciutto)

Grissini (bread sticks)

A few olives

Wrap pieces of authentic Parma Ham (prosciutto) around Grissini bread sticks as an easy-to-eat, tasty appetizer. I recommend good quality Parma Ham from the delicatessen.

Place the olives on the plate. Prepare only minutes before the arrival of your guests to keep the bread sticks crisp.

    We enjoyed this simple, but classy opener at a dinner party one evening in the home of Aurora, Giovanni, and their beautiful children. The "grissini's" were just a prelude to a seven-course Milanese meal that Mike and I left with loosened belts. Giovanni, with his unforgettable fiery eyes, had been a truck driver and union steward before starting his own office cleaning company. With charm and warmth he offered some of the most refined hospitality we experienced in Milan. And lovely Aurora made us a meal that now, many years later, I still remember vividly.

    Our evening with Aurora and Giovanni displayed so well the overwhelming graciousness Italians bring to their culinary traditions. In Lombardy, the rich region around Milan, it was difficult to know from their appearance and style a butler from a banker. Dressed up as they went out to eat, everyone looked fashionable. And in the most humble home you might have a "Babette's Feast," one that served your stomach and your eye.

    Many years later we attended a wedding in the mountains of Umbria. The lovely bride and handsome groom were neither butlers nor bankers, but at the luncheon afterwards we dined like Counts and Countesses. We mistakenly thought we were finished after they served the appetizer and pasta dishes. However they kept bringing us one sumptuous dish after another for four hours. While Mike and I enjoyed these delicious plates, eating more than we knew we should, our minds wandered back to that charming evening with Giovanni, Aurora, and their family. Times and people change, but traditions remain.

Samosas

from the South African kitchen

Servings: 10-12

I love to offer Samosas while guests chat before sitting at the table. You can also serve them as part of a buffet dinner, or for a meal that might have South African Bobotie, curry, or other Asian dishes as the main course. (See the recipe for Bobotie on page 70.)

- 1 medium Onion, finely chopped
- 3 medium Garlic Cloves, minced
- 2 Tbs Garam Masala
- 1 Tbs Ground Coriander
- 1 pkg Spring Roll Pastry (fillo pastry also works, though it's a bit more work)
- 1 ½ cups Vegetable Oil
- 1 tsp Yellow Food Coloring (optional)
- 4 Tbs Mint, fresh
- 1 lb Ground Beef
- Salt
- 1 tsp Cumin
- 1 tsp Turmeric
- 1 tsp Cilantro
- 1 Tb Zaatar* (optional)
- 4 Tbs Flour
- 1-2 Tbs Water

Fry the sliced onions in a pan with just enough oil to cover the bottom. While they brown add the ground beef (which preferably has been ground twice). Stir in the garam masala, yellow food coloring, and spices (coriander, fresh mint, garlic, cumin, cilantro, turmeric, and zatar) and salt and pepper to taste. Simmer for about 5 minutes and turn off heat.

Combine the flour and water in a separate bowl to make a semi-thick paste and put aside.

Take one sheet of spring roll pastry and cover the rest with a towel to keep them from drying out. (You can also use lumpia, a Filipino pastry, or make your own). Cut the sheet into three even parallel strips. Place about one tablespoon of the filling at the end of each strip. Then start folding from that corner diagonally across to the other side of the strip, folding the triangle downward, and continuing in this fashion until the strip is completely folded (in the same way an American flag is folded into a triangle). When the strip is completely folded, use your fingertip or a brush and place a small amount of the flour paste on the edge to seal it closed on the final side. Take another leaf, cut into strips, fill and fold, and so on until finished.

In a frying pan deep-fry the folded samosas in the hot vegetable oil until brown. Cover with a paper towel. Drain off the excess oil. (You can make the samosas ahead of time, freeze, and then defrost and fry just before serving.)

Note: Zaatar is a Middle Eastern spice found in some specialty stores. It is a mixture of thyme, sumac, and sesame seeds. You can also make your own zaatar.

Samosas are popular in multi-racial South Africa, where black tribes, "coloreds," Asians, Indians, and at least two white tribes (English and Afrikaners) all call home. When we arrived on assignment at the American Embassy some months before the historic democratic election of 1994, however, tensions among many of these groups were high. Today we know that the transition took place smoothly, but there were a lot of heroes and victims along its path. When the election was over, the people felt a strong sense of pride that their country had succeeded. I remember driving through Krueger National Park, a game preserve the size of Massachusetts, shortly after the election. There, at a rest stop, we saw a large African woman proudly wearing a T-shirt that read, "In the New South Africa, I am 'boss.'" That, and her warm smile, said it all.

Long before the election, however, the country's many ethnic groups had already mixed their many food traditions into a delicious cuisine. The Asians and Indians around Durban had many colorful and spicy dishes from the East. Walking through the booths of an outdoor market in Durban was a real experience – you found everything needed for any job, from witch-doctoring to making samosas.

This is a very nice recipe for making samosas (forget the witch-doctoring!) that came from the family recipes of a South African friend. We found that South Africans liked to make them large in size.

Spinach Pie *("Spanakopita")*
from my own kitchen, Greece

Servings: 15 on the buffet table
or 6-8 as a first course appetizer

Spinach Pie, or "spanakopita," is an exquisite Greek dish that works equally well as an appetizer, a first course, or on the buffet table. I have a lot of spanakopita recipes from Greek friends, but this is my husband, Mike's, favorite. I combined the best ingredients and techniques from several of the recipes, and this is what I discovered.

- 2 lbs Spinach, fresh
- 2 tsp Salt
- ½ cup Olive Oil
- 1 Yellow Onion, chopped
- 4 Shallots, chopped (optional)
- 3 Eggs
- 12 oz Feta Cheese, grated or crumbled
- ¼ cup Parmesan Cheese, grated
- Black Pepper
- 1 cup Butter, melted, or Olive Oil (or a mixture of half of each)
- 8 oz Fillo Sheets, (half a 16 oz. package)
- 6 Tbs Sesame Seeds
- Dill, a large bunch
- Chives, a good bunch

Put the spinach in a colander and sprinkle with salt. I like to use spinach which has been triple washed. Let the spinach stand while you sauté the onion and shallots in a large pan. Add the spinach and begin to fry it. If you have a large enough pan you can add all your spinach at once, but I add the spinach in smaller portions. While the spinach cooks and shrinks I keep slowly adding more until the entire quantity is in the pan.

When the spinach has cooked, remove it from the stove and let it cool a bit. Now add the chopped dill to the spinach mixture. Beat the eggs, mix them with the cheeses. When mixed well, I add some pepper (if you have a grinder, it is better to use fresh pepper). Then I mix everything together with the spinach.

Grease the bottom of a 13" x 9" Pyrex dish or similar type of dish with butter or olive oil. Open your fillo pastry on a clean towel and cover it with another towel that is moistened to keep it from drying out.

Take half of the pastry, about 11-12 sheets, and start to assemble them one-by-one on the dish, brushing each sheet with butter or olive oil. Now add the spinach filling and finish by placing the rest of the fillo sheets on top of the spinach in the same way. I like to use olive oil to brush the sheets, but the top sheets I brush generously with the melted butter. I notice that this gives the pie a nice brown color.

Sprinkle plenty of sesame seed on the top of the pie. Cut the pie with a sharp knife into square serving pieces before baking. I was also told by a Greek friend to sprinkle a little bit of water. This prevents the sheets from curling.

Bake the pie at 400 F until golden brown. Usually it takes about 40-45 minutes.

Spanakopita is often served alongside several other appetizers that everyone at the table shares. These starter dishes – cheese pies (*tiropites*), meat balls (*keftedes*), fried zucchini (*kolokithakia*), eggplant salad (*melanzana salata*) and many more -- are in my opinion the best part of Greek cuisine. In fact, often when visiting the taverna we order a table full of only appetizers and finish the evening happy and satisfied. I normally avoid the "mixed appetizer" selection ("poikileia") that Greek restaurants inside and outside Greece often have on the menu, because I believe they are too touristy. It is worth taking some time going through the menu and choosing your own.

In Athens, on the islands, and elsewhere, summer evenings at the taverna are busy. The dinner usually begins after 9:00 and often runs to midnight and after. One such evening, we had a delicious meal with our friends Effie and George in this colorful country taverna near Athens.

I wanted a picture to remember it, but while I was leveling my camera, a macho Greek man looked up and assumed I was taking it of him. He smiled and waved, so I waved back. That was a mistake. He tried to connect with me all evening, even with my husband there. I acted like I didn't notice when he got up to leave. Two minutes later I found him standing outside the window next to me blowing a kiss good-bye!

Strawberry Salsa

from "Dr. Yum's kitchen," Virginia

Serves 20-30

There are many Strawberry Salsa recipes around. Although similar, this one is fundamentally different: it's been tailor-made by "Dr. Yum," a pediatrician working with child nutrition and obesity problems. This recipe is healthy and nutritious and at the same time delicious. In fact a panel of child food tasters gives it thumbs up (a "Super Yum" rating), and I must say it is absolutely fantastic, definitely "Super Yum!" and not just for children.

Nimali ("Dr. Yum")

- 2 Kiwi fruit, diced
- 2 Tbs Fruit Preserves, any flavor
- 2 Golden Delicious Apples, cored and diced
- 1-2 Tbs Mint, chopped
- 8 oz Raspberries, chopped
- 1 lb Strawberries, diced
- Cooking Spray
- 6-10 Whole Grain or Spinach Tortillas
- Cinnamon
- Sugar

Preheat oven to 350 degrees. Mix fruits and preserves, cover and chill for at least 15 minutes.

Coat one side of the tortillas with cooking spray. Flip, spray again, and LIGHTLY dust with cinnamon and sugar.

Cut into wedges and arrange on a large baking sheet. Now bake for 8-10 minutes in a 350 degree oven.

Remove and cool for 2-3 minutes. Serve with the salsa.

My own grandson testers gave highest ratings: 4-year old Gabriel said "Tastes as good as cupcakes!" and 2-year old Joshua said "Actions are better than words."

    Can food be healthy and nutritious, and still attract children? I think we all wonder sometimes, but Dr. Nimali Fernando told us yes when she spoke to a group of us. And this recipe proves it.

    Nimali is a pediatrician who makes it her mission to fight nutrition and obesity problems among children. She started a website called "Dr. Yum" (www.doctoryum.com) where she gives out healthy recipes proofed by her child tasting panel. I asked Nimali if she would speak to a church women's group about the Dr. Yum project, and we came away wiser, energized, and well fed. Many of us brought refreshments made from her website recipes, and this one, Strawberry Salsa, was a huge hit.

    I find her heroic in her spirit and creative nutrition campaign. She put a kitchen in her clinic where she gives free classes on healthy cooking and other topics to anyone wishing to attend. She visits restaurants convincing many to list nutritious dishes, especially for children, and much more.

    I knew for certain that Nimali came from a long tradition of fine nutritious cooking. She is also the daughter of my good friend Kamala, many of whose excellent Sri Lankan recipes appear in *The Nomad Chef* – just proving the old proverb that the apple doesn't fall far from the tree.

Trout Mousse

from Peter's kitchen, Greece

Servings: 12

This is an excellent starter or dish for the buffet table. It's both attractive and delicious, and you can easily freeze any leftovers.

Peter

- 8 oz Smoked Trout or Salmon
- ½ Onion, grated (or Onion Flakes)
- ½ cup Mayonnaise
- 1 Egg Yolk
- 1 envelope Knox Gelatin
- ¼ cup White Wine
- 1 cup Whipped Cream

Mash the trout by hand. Grate in the onion. Mix in the mayonnaise and egg yolk. In a pan heat the wine and add to it the gelatin envelopes. Add this along with the cream that has been whipped to the fish mixture.

Now, place everything into a large mold and let it set. To remove the mold, put it into very hot water counting to nine, and immediately pop the mousse onto a platter.

Decorate the mousse surrounded with lettuce leaves and sliced avocados.

    When I go through old recipes written 20 years ago on paper that is now starting to turn yellow, I regret that I didn't write them then with better care, with clearer handwriting, and a more detailed description. There is always importance in writing down everything that is valuable when people are still alive and around you.

    This is especially true in regards to the recipes I received from Peter who had such a gift and talent for cooking. I am grateful that at least I can now share what I learned from him. He worked for the finest families in Athens, for people of many different nationalities, and for me. But he lived alone and died alone. It would be pity if no one had written down Peter's kitchen. I honor him with these recipes.

    I tell more about Peter with some of my other recipes in *The Nomad Chef*.

Asparagus in White Sauce

Servings: 4

from Peter's kitchen, Greece

This is a delightful opening dish, another of Peter's recipes (I have more than one of Peter's recipes in The Nomad Chef). You can prepare it for dinner or lunch, or simply as a lovely starter for you and a friend.

Peter

- 1 can Asparagus (about 16 oz)
- 4 slices Toast Bread, white or whole wheat
- 4 Tbs Butter
- 4 Tbs Flour
- 1 tsp Salt
- ¼ tsp Pepper
- 2 cups Asparagus liquid (or for a richer taste, use 1 cup cream, half and half, or milk)
- Olive Oil

A good thing about this recipe is that you definitely have to use canned asparagus, and that is available all year around. You will use the liquid from the asparagus for the sauce - this is the key to its good taste.

Make an ordinary white sauce by melting butter in saucepan over low heat. Blend in the flour, salt and pepper. Cook on low, stirring until smooth and bubbly. Remove from heat. Stir in 2 cups of asparagus liquid. Heat to a boil, stirring constantly. Cook and stir 1 minute.

Cut your bread slices diagonally in two and fry them just a couple of minutes in oil. Set the pieces on paper towels to eliminate extra oil. Now arrange your plates. Set the asparagus pieces in the middle and cover them lightly with the sauce. Set the bread slices around the plate. It's ready to enjoy!

If you want to vary the recipe you may add pre-cooked shrimp to your sauce. And decorate the sides of the plates with boiled egg slices. You will still use the toast as well. Pretty and tasty.

    Working with Peter was great fun! I always looked forward to those days he was in my kitchen - laughing, teasing, and mentoring. Peter was a free-lance chef and butler, and was very popular. I had to compete for his time. I normally succeeded in getting him only once a month.
    Peter had his demands, though. I had to make him Finnish pumpernickel bread, one loaf for the party and one for him to take home (you will find the pumpernickel recipe elsewhere in *The Nomad Chef*). He loved having it for breakfast with a cup of coffee and orange marmalade.

Chickpea Polenta

from Simone's kitchen, Italy

Servings: 5

I got the idea for this recipe in Venice. But "chickpea" polenta is Sicilian - one that my chef, Simone, worked up for me after I described the polenta we had at the canal-side restaurant and original Harry's Bar. It was an unforgettable evening. And if you enjoy polenta, you won't forget Simone's delightful adaptation.

Simone

- 1 2/3 cups Water
- 1 ½ pounds Chickpea Flour (Garbanzo Flour)
- 2 tsp Fennel Seed or Cumin Powder
- ½ cup Sunflower Oil or other kind of oil

Place the water in a pot with salt and bring it to a boil. When it boils, pour the chickpea meal through a sifter into the water whisking the entire time with a beater to prevent lumping. Add the fennel (or cumin). Continue to cook on a low heat for 7-8 minutes, stirring faithfully.

Shape the polenta into a roll and place it into an oblong shaped greased loaf pan. Don't leave any air bubbles inside. Cover the pan with plastic clear wrap and put it into the refrigerator to cool. When the polenta mixture is cold, remove it carefully from the loaf pan without breaking it. Slice it into ½ inch thick pieces. You can cut each slice into circles, squares, diamonds, and triangles. Fry them on both sides in a frying pan with oil. Make sure the pieces have a nice golden color so that they have a crispy texture on the surface.

Display the pieces attractively, 4 pieces on a plate and spread some fresh homemade tomato sauce on top of them. Decorate with basil.

Homemade tomato sauce
Make your own sauce from canned or fresh tomatoes, basil, salt, pepper, and a little white cooking wine. If you use fresh tomatoes (preferably cherry tomatoes) add just a bit of water; if canned, make sure to cut the tomatoes if they are whole. Put everything together in a sauce pan and cook for 20 minutes. Add some olive oil at the end.

      This recipe was born when we were in Venice visiting our friends, Franco and Lamya. Franco was head of pediatrics at the Vatican's children's hospital in Rome. Lamya, his lovely wife, was from Kuwait. She represented her country in the United Nations agencies based in Rome.
      It was a magical summer weekend, when all the boats were out. Standing on Franco's and Lamya's balcony, we watched the *festa* begin as an endless file of small, large, and long boats crowded with young people paraded down the Grand Canal below and into the Lagoon. At one point, we joined in as Franco captained us, too, into the Lagoon to watch the evening fireworks. To get a place with a view, you had to be there by 7:30, and soon there were literally thousands of boats, so close that they had to lash themselves together. The fireworks didn't start until 11:30, so there

was a lot of time for everyone to laugh and socialize. While we waited, the music grew louder, and the party bigger.

Finally, the fireworks began. They were magnificent. We had seen some impressive displays before, such as the 1976 bicentennial fireworks on the mall in Washington, DC, but this was one of the best. It was well after midnight when Franco unlashed his boat from the others. What a midnight traffic jam in the center of the lagoon it was!

Another evening we ate a marvelous meal at Harry's Bar. Our first course was polenta made with corn meal. I enjoyed the dish so much that when I got back to Rome I asked my chef Simone if he could make it. Simone said he had something even better from Sicily – similar to what ate at Harry's Bar, but from chickpeas. This is what he made. I hope you enjoy it as much as we did.

Lasagna with Radicchio

("Lasagne al Radicchio Rosso")
from the kitchen of "Pasta e Uova" in Rome

Servings: 6

This Lasagne al Radicchio Rosso" recipe was from the shop "Pasta e Uova" next to the Testaccio market in Rome. It is more elaborate than some of my others, but it is a prize well worth the effort. It is a unique "queen" of all lasagnas, and it is vegetarian as well!

- 16 oz Lasagna Noodles
- 16 oz Radicchio
- 1 qt Cream (Half and Half or a combination of the two)
- 4 oz Grated Parmesan Cheese
- 4 Tbs Extra Virgin Olive Oil
- ½ Onion
- 2 Carrots, sliced
- 2 Vegetable Broth cubes
- 2 Tbs Flour
- Salt, pepper

For lasagna noodles, if you make your own:

- 16 oz. Flour
- 3 Eggs
- Salt, Pepper

Note. You may want to bake this dish on the previous day, or if you plan to serve it on the same day, make sure it has a chance to rest ½ hour before serving. Also, if you find it too rich, use half milk and half cream.

Making lasagna noodles
You can buy good lasagna noodles in your supermarket, but here is a method for making your own: Mix all the ingredients together in a bowl forming it into a ball. Cover with a cloth and let it sit for 30 minutes. Afterwards, flatten the dough with a rolling pin into a thin layer of pasta. Cut it into 20 ½ inch strips.

Cooking the noodle
In a large pot, bring water to a boil, add salt and little oil, and put five pasta strips at a time in the water. Allow 2-3 minutes for cooking. Drain and run them through cold water. Place them on a cloth to dry, and continue until all the strips are cooked.

Preparing the radicchio filling
Cut the radicchio into small slices, rinse, and place on a cloth. Thinly slice the half onion and place in a pan with 2 tablespoons of oil. Sauté at a medium temperature. Add the carrots, radicchio, and vegetable broth cubes. Cook for approximately 20 minutes. Add 2 tablespoons of flour and 1 quart heavy cream (half and half, or a combination of cream, milk, and half and half, depending on how rich you want your sauce) a little at a time. Salt and pepper to taste. Stir frequently until it comes to boil. Lower the heat and cook for another 5 minutes until the sauce thickens.

Mixing and cooking the lasagna
Spray a ceramic oven dish (about 8" x 8") with oil. Then, place 5-6 tablespoons of the mixture on the bottom. Add a layer of the pasta squares. Then cover with another layer of the radicchio mixture. Sprinkle with grated Parmesan cheese. Continue layering in this order until you have used up all the ingredients, with the mixture. Sprinkle the final layer with Parmesan.

Preheat the oven to 400 F. Bake for 20-25 minutes. Towards the end of the cooking time raise the temperature a little. Stay by the stove and keep an eye on your lasagna until it gets a nice golden color and crispy on top.

We ate this delicious lasagna as a first course in the home of our friends Barbara and Jeff who worked as the agricultural attaché at the American Embassy in Rome. I loved its full rich flavor, and when seconds were offered I felt embarrassed, but had to have another helping. I wasn't embarrassed, though, to ask for the recipe afterwards. Barbara promised it to me, but the recipe never arrived. When Barbara and Jeff came on a return invitation to dinner at our home, I asked her to bring the recipe along.   That evening, Barbara, with a sly smile, handed me a calling card for a shop called "Pasta e Uova" ("Pasta and Eggs").

The card was Barbara's recipe. She also promised to take me to one of the Rome's best markets next to Pasta e Uova, the Testaccio market. It was only a 10-minute bus ride from my house, and I was surprised that I had already lived in the city a year and a half without learning of Testaccio.

When I arrived at Pasta e Uova I found a busy shop known for its oven ready dishes and fresh pasta. Occasionally Pasta e Uova hosted TV shows reporting the shop's traditional and tasty dishes. For once, I was a little shy to ask for the recipe, and in the beginning the owners were not too enthusiastic. With my Finnish-Karelian chatty attitude, which seemed to match the Roman joy of talking, I finally got an invitation to come back a week later. I made three trips to the shop, and eventually came away with a nicely printed recipe complete with a photograph of their kitchen. I was delighted with what they had printed on the top, for it expressed so well my own philosophy of the kitchen. It read:

The Kitchen of Pasta e Uova in Rome

"From ancient times recipes have been handed down from generation to generation. These traditional recipes are exquisite. These delicacies live in homemade cooking. Nowadays, machines help to produce and perfect the product. But the quality depends on creativity and on high-quality ingredients together with passion and good taste. For this reason we present you this old recipe with wishes of "Buon Appetito."

Lasagna Romana

from Simone's kitchen, Italy

Servings: 8 large helpings

There are so many different kinds of lasagnas, and this is an especially good one to use as a variation for our ever-roaming taste buds. Normally, lasagnas require Béchamel sauce, but this is a wonderfully light lasagna with a sweet soft taste. It is a good everyday dish along with a green salad and fresh bread. I learned it from my Italian chef Simone.

Simone

- 1 Tb Extra Virgin Olive Oil
- ¾ tsp Salt
- 2 lbs Ground Beef
- 22 oz Canned Tomatoes (any Italian brand Passata Pomodoro or Pomi strained tomatoes, is best)
- 2 cups Wine, red or white, dry*
- 9 oz (or slightly less) Lasagna Noodles, pre-cooked or ordinary
- 1 lb Mozzarella, cut into small pieces, or shredded
- 8 oz Parmesan Cheese, grated
- Some Italian spices such as oregano, thyme, or marjoram

Sauce
Fry the ground beef in the olive oil, breaking it into small pieces, until browned. Then add the wine and cook the mixture until the wine evaporates. (If you wish your sauce slightly less rich, use 1 cup wine and 1 cup water.) Add the tomatoes, salt, and spices. Cook the sauce until it thickens, about 30-40 minutes, or until it decreases by half.

Lasagna Noodles
Cook the noodles according to the package directions. It is not necessary to use pre-cooked noodles, but if you do I prefer to cook them at least 3 minutes for best results. Put your cooked noodles into a large container of cold water. After rinsing, pick them up carefully and dry well on towels.

Assembly
In a regular Pyrex dish put:
    1st, a thin layer of tomato/meat sauce
    2nd, a layer of noodles
    3rd, again, a layer of tomato/meat sauce
    4th, a layer of sliced mozzarella
    5th, a layer of parmesan cheese

and then a second time:
> 1st, a layer of noodles
> 2nd, a layer of tomato/meat sauce
> 3rd, a thin layer of parmesan cheese
> 4th, a good layer of mozzarella

Bake the dish in a 350 F oven until the cheeses are melted and the noodles have time to cook, about 30 minutes. You might want to broil the dish for a few seconds at the end to get a nice brown color, if it doesn't have one already.

    Lasagna is one of my kitchen's most versatile dishes. It actually gets better after sitting a day or two in the refrigerator, so you can make it in advance. It also freezes well for future use.
    I serve lasagna as a light first course or a full meal. Or, it is great for a buffet dinner alongside a selection of other dishes. Lasagna also transports well, making it perfect for taking to the homes of friends who need a ready meal, after the arrival of a new-born, when ill or grieving, or just to make them happy.

Pasta Sauce - Red with Sausage

Servings: 4

from the kitchen of an Italian neighbor

This rich tomato and sausage sauce is authentic and pleasant with any pasta, but is at its best over gnocchi. I am including below a gnocchi recipe in case you want to make your own.

- 1 Small Onion, chopped
- 1 Garlic Clove, minced
- Olive Oil
- ¼ cup Parsley, chopped
- 10-12 oz. Italian Sweet Sausage
- ½ cup Wine, white or red
- 6 fresh Sage Leaves (or ½ palm full dried)
- 1 sprig Rosemary (or ½ palm dried)
- 1 6-oz can Tomato Paste
- Salt and Pepper
- 1 cup Water

Chop the onion very finely and mince garlic. Fry slowly with the olive oil to soften and get some color. If the sausage has skin, remove it. If it is a long link, I cut it with kitchen scissors. Fry the sausage and then mix with parsley and onions in a pot.

Now stir the tomato sauce well into the mixture. Blend in your wine, sage leaves and rosemary. Add a cup (or more if needed) of water. Simmer about 10 minutes. Check the seasoning and add salt and pepper.

P.S. I cut the fresh rosemary with scissors, or make the needles smaller in my food processor.

Italians often told us Italy's wealthiest city and commercial center Milan was impersonal and its people were difficult to know. But when you got into the homes of the Milanese, whether they were engineers, bankers, or truck drivers, you found wonderfully refined culinary traditions.

I received this tasty Red Sauce years ago from an Italian neighbor in Milan - so many years back that I simply have lost her name. I had a chance to meet her only because we found ourselves outside in the morning waiting together for the school bus. We began to chat and once we were acquainted, I not only found a new friend (whose parents owned a restaurant!), but I got to know this excellent dish as well. I haven't found a gnocchi sauce like it anywhere.

Just to be complete, I have included a Gnocchi recipe, even though you can buy frozen gnocchi at many supermarkets. But if you want to make the gnocchi yourself, this is my Roman chef Simone's recipe.

Gnocchi

Servings: 6

Gnocchi is a treat in Italy. It is made from potatoes and eaten like pasta. In many restaurants you can get it only on Thursdays. Italians also often serve gnocchi with a four-cheese sauce, gorgonzola cheese and butter, or Genovese-style with salvia and butter. To achieve the best results, it is important to use the right kind of potato. The best are Russet potatoes which are low in water and high in starch.

3 qts Water

2 lbs Potatoes

2 lbs Flour

Salt

Boil the potatoes in their skins in salted water. Drain and peel them. Mash well (a food mill does a good job). Add the flour to the mashed potatoes. Make the mixture into long sausage-shaped rolls with a diameter of about ½ inch. Slice the rolls into pieces of about ¼ inch. Press the pieces down lightly with a fork to give a nice design. Set the pieces on a floured surface.

In a large saucepan, bring the water to a boil. Add salt and then the gnocchi six at a time. As soon as the gnocchi comes to the surface, remove from the water with a slotted spoon. Mix immediately with the sauce and serve right away while hot. (You can decorate the sauce with fresh basil leaves.)

Now, if you don't want to use all your gnocchi at the same time, you can spread the remaining pieces on a tray in a single layer and put them in the freezer. After they have frozen you can separate them, put them into individual freezer bags, and seal the sacks for future use.

The artistic lines and busy complexity of Milan's Duomo could not better portray the Milanese community surrounding the majestic cathedral

Pasta Sauce with Tomato & Basil Seirvngs: 2
from Luana's kitchen, Italy

Are you on a diet? Then this is what you should eat instead of creamy pasta sauce. Tomato Sauce with Fresh Basil, or "Salsa di Pomodoro con Basilico Fresco" as Luana called it, is an easy, simple, and authentic Italian folk kitchen recipe for a delicious pasta sauce. Serve it on top of your favorite spaghetti, noodles, or pasta, and of course, sprinkle grated parmesan over the sauce.

Luana

Olive Oil

1 lb Cherry Tomatoes

Basil, fresh, whole bunch

2 Garlic Cloves

Salt

Wash and halve your tomatoes. (You can substitute other mid-sized tomatoes with a good flavor for the cherry tomatoes.)

In a pan that has 1 tablespoon of olive oil, sauté the garlic pieces. Add your tomatoes and cook about 10 minutes, stirring every now and then. Now, throw in your washed fresh basil, a good handful (if not available, you can use dried basil. Let it cook about 10 minutes more. No water is needed because your tomatoes will have liquid of their own. Salt at the end, according to taste. Italians add olive oil.

Using fresh tomatoes instead of tomato pastes or sauces is important for red sauces. If fresh tasty tomatoes are not available you can use a large can (about a pound) of tomatoes. In this case I cut the tomatoes into small pieces. Otherwise follow the rest of the recipe.

Luana, our housekeeper in Rome gave this recipe to me. When we departed, Luana went to work for the French embassy as one of the housekeepers in Villa Farnese, the French ambassador's residence. This exquisite Renaissance palace of the Farnese family, with its architecture, paintings, and sculptures, is one of the world's great treasures. I could only imagine what it must be like to work each day in such a place.

On one visit to Rome, Mike and I were staying at a wonderful small hotel on Campo di Fiori, which connected to Piazza Farnese, the square in front of the palace. One look at Villa Farnese, and I knew I had to find Luana. I marched inside its tall heavy doors, Mike two steps behind, and I told the receptionists who were surrounded by several guards, that I had come to see Luana. They mumbled something, and finally said she was away on summer vacation. I persisted, asking when she was getting back, and so on. Finally, someone replied, "Momento!" and in two minutes Luana was standing right there, delighted to see us. She took us up the long staircase, designed by Michelangelo, and we were in the middle of the French Ambassador's reception rooms. Fortunately for us, he was away, so we received a private tour.

We have been back to our favorite hotel on Campo di Fiori. I look out the window of our room, never knowing what to expect: in the mornings, the market stalls full of shoppers, or the beautiful palace along the way, once the filming of a Woody Allen film, and, of course, always couples in love.

Villa Farnese

Pasta Sauce – White

from my own kitchen

Servings: 2 ½ cups sauce

Pasta and Italy are almost synonymous, but I found a down-side to spending five years in Italy where we ate heavenly pastas daily. It is now hard for me to appreciate pasta sauces that are so often made with too little care in restaurants outside Italy. So I make my pastas at home, and I've included some excellent pasta recipes in The Nomad Chef. This one I developed myself. It has the rich zesty flavor found on good pastas in Italy and is easy to make. It is a winner on any kind of pasta, both long pastas (such as, spaghetti, linguini, and vermicelli) or smaller pastas (such as, shells, rigatoni, and tortiglioni).

There are a few secrets to good pasta sauces. Grated real Italian parmesan cheese ("Grana Reggiano" or "Grana Padano") is a must if you want the best flavor, especially in white sauces.

- ¼ cup Butter
- ¼ cup Flour
- 1 ½ cups Chicken Broth
- 2 Tbs Sherry (optional)
- ½ cup Whipping Cream, whipped
- ½ cup Parmesan Cheese, grated

First whip the cream and the set it aside.

Melt the butter in a saucepan, add flour to it, and mix it well. Cook over low heat until it thickens. Remove from the heat and stir in slowly the chicken broth. Heat to boiling, and boil 1-2 minutes.

Now, remove the sauce from stove and stir in the sherry and parmesan cheese. Let cool, and then fold in whipped cream.

Pasta al Mare

from Luana's kitchen, Italy

Servings: 4

This is one of my favorite pasta recipes, maybe because I am such a fan of seafood. I like it also because it is relatively low calorie for a pasta.

Luana

- 8-10 oz Pasta Noodles or Spaghetti
- Olive Oil
- 2 Garlic Cloves, crushed
- 1 Fresh Red Pepper, chopped
- 10 Red Pepper flakes
- 12-15 Cherry Tomatoes, halved
- 1 Tb Basil, dried, 4-5 fresh leaves
- 1 lb Seafood (Clams, Prawns, Octopus)
- 1 cup White Wine, dry
- Italian Parsley, fresh
- Salt, Pepper

Sauté the chopped and cleaned red pepper along with the garlic in the olive oil. When the pepper softens a little, add the seafood, a small amount at a time, and stir. You can use clams, prawns, octopus, or a combination of them. Now, add the tomatoes, pepper flakes, and basil. Cover your pan with a lid and let it cook slowly about 15 minutes. Remove the lid and add the white wine. Cook slowly again for about 10 minutes without a lid. Salt and pepper. At the end of the cooking add your cleaned and chopped parsley. Stir for about 1 minute.

Meanwhile you have cooked your pasta (spaghetti, fettuccini, or linguini) according to directions (8-10 ounces for 4 people is a generous helping). Add the seafood sauce to your ready cooked pasta. Mix it around in the pot until well blended.

Just before eating, Italians add a little more olive oil and top with plenty of fresh parsley. However, they don't put parmesan on fish pastas, and in a restaurant if you ask for parmesan to top a fish pasta, you are likely to get a cross look from the waiter, and maybe even some counseling.

Luana, my housekeeper, said that she was not a cook -- but she still managed to keep her Italian family alive and well fed for over 20 years. She was like the rest of the Italians. They appreciate fine dishes and almost instinctively know how to make them.

My husband claims that if you scratch an Italian, you will find Michelangelo underneath. Anything artistic comes naturally. Art and beauty are everywhere. As you wander through Rome, you are overwhelmed with layers of beauty atop each other.

So it was with Luana. We both loved Michelangelo and talked about him while preparing this wonderful seafood pasta. I have served it to company and always received rave reviews.

Risotto con Erbe

Servings: 3 - 4

from the kitchen of the Orazio Restaurant in Rome

This herb risotto is unbelievably good, and it is healthy. I received the recipe from the Orazio Restaurant that sits in the ancient center of Rome.

Orazio's Head Waiter with Mary Lou and myself

- 1 cup Rice, preferably Carolina or Arborio
- 1 qt warm Vegetable or Chicken Broth (more if needed)
- 1 Tb Butter
- 3 tsp Extra-Virgin Olive Oil
- 1/4 lb Asparagus, preferably fresh
- 1/4 lb Spinach, preferably fresh
- 1 ½ cups Parmesan Cheese, freshly grated
- ½ - 1 cup Cream
- 2 Tbs Fennel Seeds

First clean your spinach and asparagus, and then boil each of them in separate pans with just enough water to cover. Remove the vegetables with a strainer spoon and puree them in a blender or hand mill. Set aside. You can save the vegetable liquid to use in place of the vegetable or chicken broth if you wish.

Heat the oil and butter in a large saucepan over medium-low. Add the rice and fennel seeds and sauté, stirring for 1 to 2 minutes until the mixture begins to color. Lower the heat, ladle in enough warm broth to cover the rice, and continue to stir until the broth has thickened. Add the pureed vegetable mix. Stir. Continue cooking by adding more broth, one ladle at a time every 5 minutes or so, stirring occasionally, until the rice is *al dente* (soft, but not mushy) and the risotto is dense, about 30 minutes in total.

At the end, add the cream and 4 heaping tablespoons of Parmesan cheese. (Using fresh Italian parmesan makes a BIG difference). Mix thoroughly and cover. Let the risotto sit for 3 minutes. Serve at once, with a bowl of the remaining cheese on the side.

    The Orazio Restaurant in Rome rested between the ancient Caracalla Roman baths and the Colosseum – just across from the United Nations Food and Agriculture Organization where diplomats from 190 countries worked together to improve the world's food production. On a warm afternoon, as you sat in the Orazio gardens, you would see people from every part of the world, often in colorful dress. There, they gathered in deep discussions about global food questions, enjoying this and other lovely dishes from Orazio's fine menu. I always thought that the Orazio gardens had to be a big improvement over the stuffy rooms across the street. And for that matter, maybe negotiations done over pasta would improve the unresolved quest to find world peace!

    When I ate at the Orazio, I often didn't look at the menu because I knew what I wanted. I ate my risotto spoonful-by-spoonful, closing my eyes to taste its deep flavor. Relaxing in the restaurant garden, I felt healthy and strong.

    I was there one warm July afternoon with my friend Mary Lou when I finally convinced the head waiter to give me the recipe for Risotto con Erbe. Mary Lou was still recovering from the sudden loss of her wonderful husband, Bill. (Bill had provided me with design and layout suggestions for *The Nomad Chef*.) In the aftermath of his passing, we had invited Mary Lou to visit us in Rome, and that afternoon we sat in the shade of Orazio's warm gardens and enjoyed this excellent pasta dish.

Risotto Milanese

Servings: 12

from the kitchen of Signor and Signora Riva, Italy

Risotto Milanese is an excellent first course that goes especially well on the same menu with Vitello Tonnato ("Tuna'ed Veal"). But it is also rich and full and can easily be served as a course of its own rather than just as a side.

Butter

4 cups Arborio Rice

12 cups Beef Broth, warm

½ - 1 cup Parmesan Cheese

2 Medium Onions, chopped

1 cup Dry White Wine

¼ - 1 tsp Saffron

Olive Oil

Sauté the onions in olive oil until transparent. Stir in the rice and cook for about 2 minutes until it gets a golden color. Add the wine and bring to a boil. Then let everything simmer until it is absorbed.

Start adding the warm beef broth, ladle-by-ladle. Use your broth from preparing Vitello Tonnato (Tuna'ed Veal) if you are serving these two together. Otherwise, use canned broth or broth from bouillon cubes. Keep cooking and stirring until the liquid is totally absorbed, gradually adding more broth until the broth is consumed and your risotto has finally reached a soft, creamy texture. I know that in some homes, they add a touch of cream.

Dissolve saffron in a small amount of the broth. Add the saffron liquid at some point toward the end of the cooking. Stir in the Parmesan cheese and butter according to your taste.

      In many countries meals are served on a plate full of several dishes, but Italians often prefer their courses to follow one another in sequence: antipasto, first course, second course, and so on. They are very careful about mixing flavors.

      I learned this soon after we moved to our first posting in Milan, Italy. Milan was such a great place to begin expanding my culinary repertoire and develop my skills. Once, when I invited guests to a traditional American Thanksgiving meal, they loved the roast turkey, but were a little surprised at how everything was served together. The cranberry sauce, especially, raised eyebrows. We would never serve something sweet on the same dish as the main course, one of our guests told me. "A sugar dish served together with the main meal destroys the nice flavors of the other food," she said..

      I was at first taken aback by our guest's straight forward reaction, but later I started to agree. Mixing strong flavors on the same plate, especially a sugar dish such as cranberry sauce, can interfere with an appreciation of a tasty main course.

      (See my "Vitello Tonnato" recipe to learn the fun story about how I received this recipe.)

Seafood Spaghetti

from Markos's kitchen, Greece

Servings 2

If you like seafood and you like pasta, you will love this recipe. To make this spaghetti best, you should use fresh seafood

Markos

- 6 large Shrimp
- 6 Mussels
- 1 Squid
- Olive Oil
- ¼ Onion
- 1 Tb Garlic, chopped
- 2 Large Tomatoes, cut into pieces (or 8 oz. Cherry Tomatoes)
- Fresh Dill
- 2 Tbs Tomato Paste
- 1/3 cup Ouzo
- Spaghetti Noodles

Cut the squid into small pieces. Keep the mussels and shrimp whole for decoration. Cover the bottom of the frying pan with olive oil and sauté the chopped garlic and onion. When it has the color, add the seafood, including the whole shrimp, continuing to sauté and stir.

Now carefully add enough water to cover the bottom of the pan, but not to cover the seafood. When the water comes to a boil, cover it with a lid. Keep an eye on the pan and cook until the water evaporates. Take off the lid and add tomatoes, ouzo, tomato paste, and fresh dill. Cook about 2 minutes to vaporize the Ouzo's alcohol. Salt and Pepper to taste. Mix the sauce with cooked spaghetti.

Organize your dish nicely with the large whole shrimps arranged on top of each plate. Decorate with additional fresh dill, if available.

"Little Venice" on the Greek island of Mykonos

    I can always see clearly in my mind an elderly Greek widow sitting on the seaside, her long black dress pulled close to her knees, dipping her toes in the water, raising her sunburned face towards the sky, and smilingly whispering *Thalassa* ("The Sea").

So it is: nearly every Greek's passion from young to old is the sea! It's not the love of the sea, but also the wealth in their turquoise-colored waters. Greeks delight in seafood and fish, and it is expensive around the Mediterranean. The best Greeks can offer their guests are delicacies of the

sea, in their homes, restaurants, or tavernas. They are a hospitable and generous people. For friends, they serve their best, and that is fish.

Markos's Seafood Pasta comes from Mykonos, the lovely queen of the Greek islands. It has been a popular tourist spot since the early 1950's. Mykonos' shining beauty starts from its white washed buildings. The town is restored and well kept. Its Cycladic buildings are delightful. In its labyrinth of streets, we found the Avra restaurant, and I lost my heart and palate to Markos's delicious spaghetti.

Markos was a talented self-trained chef at the Avra restaurant, what I thought was one of the most enjoyable on Mykonos. "Avra" in Greek means "breeze," and that perfectly described the pleasant atmosphere on its garden terrace. Markos' wife also worked at the Avra as a waitress, and they spent the summer on the island together. Like most of the other Mykonians, they returned to Athens for winter.

For at least the past 50 years, Mykonos' mascot has been a pelican that wanders the narrow streets often crowded with people. It even pops into shops, especially those filled with the aromas of food. These days, the town may have three of these personable mascots.

The island is also known for its heavy August winds, the "Meltemi." But when you walk up and down Mykonos' narrow meandering streets you hardly know there is a wind blowing. It's easy to get lost as you wander through the town, something we always did - we wandered and we got lost. And we were always glad when we finally found our way to Markos' delightful dishes at the Avra.

Beef Tenderloin al Barolo

Servings: 2 portions

from Simone's kitchen, Italy

This is a rich and full-bodied main course. My Roman chef Simone made it for us on several memorable evenings. You can substitute another red wine for the Barolo.

Simone

- 1 lb Beef Tenderloin cut into four 1-plus inch slices
- 2 Tbs Flour
- 2 Tbs Juniper Berries
- 1 Bay leaf
- 1 cup Barolo or other robust Red Wine
- 1 Tb Extra Virgin Olive Oil
- 1 Tb Butter
- Salt and Pepper

Flour, salt, and pepper the fillet pieces. In a heavy frying pan fry them lightly on both sides. Set the meat pieces aside. Now add the wine to the drippings (if you don't have Barolo, use a hearty red wine such as Cabernet Sauvignon), juniper berries, and laurel leaf. Bring to a boil and simmer about 5-10 minutes. Adjust seasoning. Put the meat pieces back into the pan to get flavor from the sauces for 1-2 minutes. Then it's ready to serve topped with this impressive sauce.

P.S. Don't hesitate to thicken the sauce with some flour and/or corn starch if you want it thicker.

    Simone, like his Roman ancestors, never shied from elegance. And "elegance" is Beef Tenderloin al Barolo in one word. (See more about Simone in my "Orange and Olive" recipe.)
    This may seem a pricey main course, especially if you buy a bottle of Barolo, which is considered the "king of Italian wines," or sometimes, the "Italian wine of kings." However, this is how I look at it. If you go out to a good restaurant, you are likely to dine on something much less elegant than this recipe, and with tips the tab will be a lot more than you will pay if you are the chef, serving Beef Tenderloin al Barolo. Best of all, you get the credit (and maybe a kiss or two) for a delicious meal.

Bobotie

Servings: 8

from Terttu's kitchen, South Africa

I'm a Bobotie fan and this recipe from Terttu was the best Bobotie I found in South Africa. It is a dish thought to have come originally to South Africa from Indonesia. You eat it as a main course casserole, like lasagna or mousakka, and serve with rice, chutney, coconut, and bananas.

Terttu

- 1 thick slice White Bread, crust removed and cut into small pieces
- 1 ½ cups Milk
- 1 ½ Tbs Oil
- 2 tsp Butter
- 2 Onions, finely sliced
- 2 Garlic Cloves, crushed
- 1 ½ Tbs Curry Powder
- 2 tsp Salt
- 1 ½ Tbs Chutney
- 1 Tb Apricot Jam (smooth)
- 1 Tb Worcestershire Sauce
- 1 ½ Tbs Brown Vinegar
- 2 lbs Ground Beef
- ½ cup Raisins
- 3 Eggs
- Lemon or Bay Leaves

Soak the bread in the milk. Heat the oil and butter in a large frying pan and fry the onions and garlic until soft. Once soft, add the curry powder, salt, chutney, and apricot jam, Worcestershire sauce, and vinegar, and mix well. Drain the milk from the bread. Keep the milk to one side. Also, set aside separately the squeezed bread.

Fry the meat and raisins in a frying pan over a low heat, stirring continuously until the meat is no longer pink. Remove from the stove and thoroughly mix in one well beaten egg with the meat and bread. Place into an approximately 11 x 6 inch oven dish. Mix in the rest of the eggs with the milk that was kept to one side, and add a dash of salt. Pour over the meat and add a few bay or lemon leaves on top. Cover the Bobotie with aluminum foil.

It is important to prevent the meat from drying out as it bakes. To do this, you place your oven dish on top a baking pan, such as a cookie sheet, and fill the baking pan with a layer of water. Bake for 1 hour at 350 F until the dish is firm. Check occasionally to see that the water does not disappear, adding more as needed.

Serve with rice, chopped coconut, chutney, nuts and sliced banana.

How do you make your lunch or dinner unforgettable? Sometimes you don't have to do anything, like when this hippo climbed from the river in southern Africa to nap at our restaurant. Across the river an elephant kept an eye on us while we ate. The waiter warned us not to bother them. We didn't.

South-Africa comes close to paradise in many various ways due to its wonderful climate, the richness of its nature, the wild animal life, and especially, of course, its peoples and their cuisine. South-African cuisine is often called "rainbow cuisine" probably because the country is known for its ethnic and cultural diversity. Settlers transported food from many areas like The Netherlands, India, the East Indies, Britain and Portugal, and these dishes often mixed with African tastes and customs. I am a friend of all the South African dishes, but my favorite one is Bobotie, spiced minced meat with a custard topping.

I got this Bobotie recipe from Terttu, a Finnish friend whose husband Timo worked for the Finnish Embassy in Pretoria, South Africa. Our two families quickly became friends, but it wasn't just the Finnish blood that pulled us together – it was also our love of fine dishes. Bobotie was one of them.

Mike and I arrived in South Africa on assignment to the American Embassy in 1993, just a year before the historic day when Nelson Mandela was elected president. We were outsiders and maybe that helped us see how quickly a transition was taking place before us. But many South Africans were uncertain. On the radio news each morning we heard of a new bombing or other atrocity, and it was natural to feel uneasy. But a few months later when the election arrived, it happened smoothly.

A transition took place in the lives of many people. In our own home I hired Letty, the wife of our gardener Jameson, to be my housekeeper and cook. Despite being married for many years and having two boys together, Letty and Jameson never found work in the same place. They had never lived together until Letty came to live with us. Letty had never formally cooked or served a meal for a family, either. So she came to my kitchen, and we started working together. She learned quickly, and it wasn't long before she had new and marketable skills as a domestic.

Jameson had never been to a movie theater until one evening when we took him with us. At first, he felt uncomfortable surrounded by an all-white audience, but he soon relaxed to enjoy the film. And their little boy had never been to a supermarket until one afternoon when I took him along As our grocery cart approached the cash register, he saw a package with a small toy car hanging from the stall. "Car!" he exclaimed, the first word he had spoken the entire time we had been shopping. I pulled it into our cart and he had his first toy car. So life went forward, sometimes miraculously.

Criminal violence was almost everywhere. We knew many victims. For example, one evening we were hosting a dinner party and one of our Black South African guests and his wife never arrived. I was annoyed that guests seemed to simply ignore the meal I had prepared. However, Monday morning they called to apologize. Their car had been hijacked the afternoon of our dinner. In spite of their loss, they felt very fortunate to be still alive. I felt guilty to have felt unkind thoughts about them.

When after three years Mike and I sat on the plane awaiting our departure from Johannesburg, we talked about how the years had been some of the best and most exciting of our career. Then, with a deep breath, we looked at each other and agreed we would never come back to this country where we had seen so many victims.

Well, never say never. A year later we *were* back — buying a time share! And we came back to the beloved country annually for many years.

Before moving to Africa, we had heard that there was something in addition to the lovely dishes and meals that got into your blood, making it impossible ever to separate completely from the continent and its hospitable peoples. That happened to us, too

Married with two children, Jameson and Letty had never had the opportunity to live together as a family until I brought her into our home where she learned to cook in my kitchen. Their little boy had never been to a supermarket until I took him. So the transition before us was much more than political.

Cameroonian Fish with Tomato Sauce
from M'fikela's kitchen, Cameroon Servings: 4

This fish dish that I received from M'fikela is exotically spiced with curry and fresh ginger, M'fikela's recipe, however, used a delicious fish found in that part of the south Atlantic called "capitano." I have not been able to find capitano in the U.S., but the recipe works well with any tasty fish. I used mahi mahi and was very pleased.

M'fikela

- 2 lbs Fish (filleted)
- 1 Lemon
- Flour
- Olive Oil
- 1 Tb Butter
- Salt
- 6-7 fresh Tomatoes
- 1 Onion
- 2 Garlic Cloves
- 1 tsp Curry Powder
- 1 tsp Sugar
- 1 ½ inch piece Fresh Ginger

Squeeze lemon juice on both sides of the fish to get a rid of the fishy aroma. (Mahi mahi actually has very little fishy aroma). The fish preferably should be thick in flesh. Sprinkle both sides of the fish with salt, cut into 4 pieces, and let it sit for a while.

Meanwhile, peel the tomatoes and cut them into smaller chunks. (The best way to peel the tomatoes is to blanche them in boiling hot water. Before doing that, cut a little x on the top of the tomatoes, then put into the hot water for 20 seconds and wait a minute to peel them. The peel comes off easily this way.) Chop the onion, crush the garlic, and chop the ginger into small pieces. Set them aside.

Now, take the fish pieces, pat them dry with a paper towel, and roll them in flour that has some salt.

Heat ¼ inch of olive oil and butter in a large pan. When the oil is hot, fry the fish on both sides until it has a golden color and it has almost reached an interior temperature of 125 F. Drain off the extra oil by placing the fish pieces on a paper towel and set aside.

Pour 2 ½ tablespoons new oil into the pan and heat. When the oil is hot, put the onions and ginger into the pan. Sauté until they have a golden color. Now add the tomatoes, curry powder, and sugar.

Adjust the salt. Bring the mixture to a boil, and then lower the heat to medium or less. Cover the pan, stirring now and then for about 20 minutes. Add the fish carefully, not to break the pieces. Let simmer for 5 minutes. Serve with basmati rice.

M'fikela worked for diplomatic families living in Cameroon's capital, Yaoundé. When we met her, she was cooking for our diplomat son's family. What a refined and versatile person M'fikela was. She handled our four energetic grandsons, all under seven, like a grandmother at the same time she was cooking and serving dishes fit for any occasion – big or small.

M'fikela followed in the tradition of so many African women who are the lifeblood and strong backs of their communities. During one of his official trips to Africa, Mike visited a small farm in Zimbabwe. The owner was a woman over 70. She and her daughter, who was in her fifties, cultivated a field of corn and were at ease talking about different corn varieties and their strong points. There were no men in the house helping, even with the heavy work.

Chicken with Lemon and Oil

Servings 2

from Concetta's kitchen, Sicily

We can take many lessons from a lovely lemon tree. It is very pretty, its flower so sweet, and its fruit is possible to eat. And if you want to fancy a very tasty dish, imagine this Sicilian lemon chicken from Concetta. It is fresh and bright, like a day of Sicilian sunshine. And best of all, it is easy - I learned just how easy it was to make as I watched Concetta effortlessly prepare it after a full day of touring Caltagirone, her beautiful town in Sicily.

Concetta

2 Chicken Breasts, boneless (about 1 ¼ lbs.)

2 Lemons

2 Tbs Butter

1 Tb Olive Oil

½ tsp Pepper

Flour

Salt

If the chicken breasts are thick, slice them length-wise into thin layers (the thinner, the better). Salt the pieces, then roll them in flour where the pepper has been added.

Heat the butter and olive oil in a frying pan (an electric frying pan works best), and wait until it gets color before adding the chicken slices. Fry on a medium heat.

While your chicken is frying, grate the peel from the top of the 2 lemons. Then squeeze the juice of one of the lemons over the slices and sprinkle with the grated lemon peel. Cook until they have a beautiful golden color on both sides, but still moist.

We met Concetta when we were visiting Sicily, the Mediterranean's largest island. She was a relative of our good Sicilian friends Maria and Amalia and lived in the town of Caltagirone. The city, which gets its name from an Arabic word meaning "the castle of the fortress of the vases," is a Baroque town where you see handmade ceramics everywhere.

Maybe the streets were not ceramic, but the street signs were, the bridge had ceramic railings, the 142 steps going up to the cathedral were covered with ceramic tile (each one different!), and many shops had ceramic facades. Inside the artisans' boutiques lining the streets were some of the most beautiful ceramic vases and tables I had ever seen. Of course I would have bought everything I saw, but my husband resisted (as is his nature). At one point I did prevail, and Mike let me choose a beautiful breakfast table with a colorful ceramic design layered over black lava from nearby Mt. Etna.

Concetta guided us through the town and shops, and that the afternoon we enjoyed a sumptuous dish when Concetta invited us to her home for dinner. Working first in her office and later spending the day with us had left Concetta little time to prepare a meal. But while we sat in her living room for maybe only 15 minutes visiting with Maria and Amalia, Concetta made us tasty chicken sautéed and flavored with lemon.

Incidentally, the ceramic top of the table we brought from Caltagirone is decorated with lemons and vines. Now, as we sit at our table, we reflect on that delightful afternoon when we ate lemon chicken at Concetta's table.

Concetta, Maria, and Amalia took us on a visit to Sicily's ceramic city Caltagirone

I love dinner parties everywhere. But nothing beats the fun of being invited to a party with families and friends in southern Europe. Our afternoon with Maria, her husband Nicola, and her family young and old was alive with energy and full of tasty dishes.

The 142 steps up to Caltagirone's cathedral were covered with thousands of unique ceramic tiles.

I would have loved to have this vase - I won't tell you how much it cost.

Even the street signs were ceramic.

A toy store was unbelievably ceramic!

The Nomad Chef

Chicken with Rosemary

Servings 4

from Ana Maria's kitchen, Spain

So much about cooking is visual, aroma, and color. This was so with Ana Maria's chicken from her home in Spain. The aroma fills your kitchen as you prepare it.

Ana Maria

- 4 Chicken Breasts, preferably thin ones
- 4 Onions (sliced)
- 3 Tbs Rosemary
- Olive Oil, enough to marinate the chicken plus a little extra to fry the onions
- 2 Tbs Butter
- Flour

Marinate the chicken pieces in a bowl with rosemary and olive oil for 3-4 hours or even longer. You may wish to grind the rosemary first into smaller pieces in a food processor or a mortar in order to give a smoother texture.

In a large pan fry the onions in butter and olive oil until they are well cooked and have a nice golden color. Set aside.

Remove the chicken from its marinating sauce and roll in flour which has salt and pepper mixed in. Now sauté the chicken in the same pan where you fried the onions. Add some of the marinating oil to the pan for the sauté process. Salt and pepper.

While the chicken is cooking place the onions in a food processor and puree them into a sauce. You can thin it with a little water if the sauce is too thick. Put the sauce into a serving bowl.

When the chicken is done, place it on a platter and serve it with the onion gravy.

    Ana Maria was a Spanish friend whom we got to know in Greece. When we first met, she astonished us by saying she knew all about us. She explained she had lived earlier in Milan, Italy, and had learned about our family from friends whom we had also known years before when we lived there. So, surprise! The world really is small. When we finally met in Athens we were like old friends.

    But that wasn't the end of this tale. The years passed, and again we met Ana Maria, but this time in the western United States where she had moved from Athens. At a reunion in her new home, we were met with the familiar tummy tickling aromas from her kitchen, and particularly this Spanish chicken dish. She had just married a charming widower. What a joy to see happiness in the eyes of "mature" people and to share our renewed friendship with a delicious meal.

    As Ana Maria tapped castanets against her fingers while taking a few dance steps and humming a folk song, her Latin personality always created a warm Spanish atmosphere.

Cottolette
from Simone's kitchen, Italy

Servings: 2-3

Italians love veal dishes. So do I, even though veal is not always readily available in many markets. But it is worth finding, and when you do try this enjoyable evening main course. Marination is the secret – it will bring out the refined flavor of the veal. My Roman chef Simone is the creator of this fine dish.

Simone

- 4 Veal Cutlets, thinly sliced, about 4 oz. each
- Corn Oil (extra light) or Olive Oil for frying
- 1-2 Tbs Butter
- 1 Egg
- 1 ½ cups Breadcrumbs
- 1 cup White Wine
- 1-2 Lemons

Marinate the veal cutlets in a wine and egg mixture for at least 2 hours. The egg should first be lightly whipped. Roll the cutlets in breadcrumbs that already have salt and pepper mixed in. If you wish, dip the cutlets again in the wine mixture and repeat coating with breadcrumbs one more time.

Now the cutlets are ready to be fried in a pan with a little hot oil and butter. Use an electric frying pan if you have one, starting out at 350 F. After they take color, turn the heat to 275 F and put on the lid. Cook until done. If you use a conventional frying pan, start at medium temperature on the stove. After the meat has color, lower the temperature, cover with a lid, and let it cook slowly. Brown on both sides and serve immediately.

Squeeze juice from the lemons over the veal.

    The first time I was introduced to Cottolette was in Milan, Italy, when our daughter Kaarina was in the hospital suffering from a concussion – one of our many trips to an Italian emergency room with our active children and their accidents. My husband and I would take turns staying in the hospital, and during my long watch, an Italian friend brought us cottolette inside panini sandwiches – one of my most welcome lunches ever. My, how I savored that Cottolette. We learned that in Italian hospitals, at least then, the family took care of bringing food to loved ones in the hospital. We had no family in Milan, but our friends, in great Italian fashion, took good care of us.   (More about Simone elsewhere in *The Nomad Chef*).

Finnish Holiday Ham
from my own recipe

There is nothing like a unique and delicious Finnish Holiday Ham ("Joulukinkku"). This recipe, adapted from a number of others I have, makes a delightful meal for your Holiday celebration. And it will be a welcome surprise, something beyond the usual holiday ham or turkey.

Ham
10 - 20 lb Fresh Ham

   Whole cloves

Brine
8 qts Water

3 cups Sugar

2 cups Coarse Salt

Rye Flour Paste
8 cups Rye Flour

   Water

Glaze
2-4 Tbs Brown Sugar

2-4 Tbs Bread Crumbs

2-4 Tbs Finnish Mustard

Finnish Style Mustard (optional)
1/3 cup Mustard Powder

1/3 cup Sugar

1/3 cup Cream

1/3 cup Egg Yolks

1 tsp Potato Starch

2 tsp Vinegar

   a dash Salt

The Ham
In Finland, Joulukinkku usually comes pre-salted, but in the United States you will use "fresh ham" that needs to soak considerably in a salt/sugar brine. The soak time can be greatly reduced by using a meat injector. I think the flavor also gains from the injector as the brine reaches deep inside the meat.

Combine the brine ingredients in a large pot and bring to a boil to dissolve the salt and sugar. Prepare the ham by making a few shallow gashes over the entire surface. Do not remove the skin. Now place the ham skin side up in a large container or bucket and cover with the brine sauce. With a meat injector inject brine into the ham in five or six different spots. Let the ham soak in the brine mixture for four days. (If you do not use a food injector, you will need to soak the ham for about two weeks.)

Prepare the ham for baking by again injecting brine throughout the ham. Mix the rye flour paste ingredients. Add enough water to make a thick dough and roll the dough into about a 1/4 inch thickness. Arrange the ham in a baking pan skin-side up and cover the ham with the rye paste.

Bake in a slow oven (250 F) 4-6 hours, depending on the size of the ham, until the internal ham temperature reaches 160 F. Keep a small amount of water in the bottom of the pan to prevent the ham from burning. When it is done, take the ham from the oven and discard the rye crust. You can also remove the skin and excess fat. Cut the ham surface with diamond shaped markings and place whole cloves in each intersection. Cover the ham with a layer of Finnish mustard. I have bought Swedish mustard - which is about the same as Finnish mustard - from Ikea, but you can easily make your own.

Finally, sprinkle with bread crumbs and brown sugar, and return the ham to a hot oven (400 F) for half an hour. After removing the ham, you can eat it hot or cold. Finns normally serve it room temperature.

Finnish Style Mustard
Blend the dry mustard and sugar. Mix in the egg yolk, cream, and potato starch. Heat to a boil, stirring continuously. Add salt and vinegar after cooling.

Santa's visit early Christmas Eve was one of many Finnish merry-making traditions in our home

    The Finland where I grew up was full of holiday traditions. The first ritual was work. Everyone was very busy getting ready for the Christmas celebration, cleaning the house, making the dishes, and getting presents ready. On Christmas Eve we cut and decorated our Christmas tree, took a Christmas sauna, and welcomed Santa - who made his rounds while the children were still awake. Christmas day we spent with our family, and Boxing Day was celebrated with friends or cross country skiing. Christmas Eve, Christmas Day, and Boxing Day were all national holidays, and so was New Year's Eve and New Year's Day. So everything came to a standstill throughout the Christmas week. In my home, New Year's Eve had its own games and customs that foretold our fortunes for the coming year.

    And we ate! My parents traditionally baked their *Joulukinkku* ham on the morning of Christmas Eve. That evening we enjoyed it with many other Finnish specialties, casseroles and delightful holiday breads. The ham stayed in the house's cold entrance hall for the night and was enjoyed again on Christmas Day, Boxing Day and many days thereafter.

Fried Chicken
from Esther's kitchen, Idaho

This is my cowboy husband's favorite chicken, not just because it is his Grandmother Esther's recipe. He says he is just a simple man and appreciates simple things. (I wish he were a little more simple, more often.) This chicken recipe is rich, but lip smacking. I haven't found one like it in any of the cookbooks, and none of the chefs who have worked in our residence over the years was ever able to replicate it from their own experience. Its secret is the long, slow cooking.

Esther

- 1-2 pieces Chicken per person
- brown paper bag
- Flour
- Butter
- Corn Oil (extra light) or olive oil for frying
- Salt and Pepper
- Poultry Seasoning

Gravy
- Milk
- Flour
- Salt and pepper

You will need a heavy frying pan with a lid or an electric frying pan (which works the best because you can control the temperature).

Pour a cup or two of flour in a paper bag and add some salt, pepper and poultry seasoning. Shake well. Coat your chicken pieces one-by-one in the paper bag shaking it to get an even coating. Melt a small chunk of butter in the oil, and when it starts bubbling in the pan you are ready to fry your chicken.

Fry the chicken pieces carefully (electric frying pan temperature 350 F, ordinary pan, medium high heat). If the oil has disappeared from the pan, you obviously need more. The meat absorbs it. When your

The secret is the long, slow cooking, and then gaining a crispy golden color at the very end.

chicken has a nice brown color on both sides, reduce the temperature in your electric frying pan to 250 or even lower. If you are frying on a stove, set the heat on low. In the electric pan, put the lid on with the steam vent closed; with a normal pan, set the lid on, but keep checking every now and then that the chicken pieces don't dry out (if they do, add oil or butter). After approximately 40 minutes the meat will have become soft and tender. Check once more to find if the chicken needs extra salt, pepper, or seasoning. Now do the final cooking without the lid to give the meat crispiness. About 6 minutes should be enough.

Gravy
Place the pieces on a platter and cover with aluminum foil and a towel to keep them warm while you prepare the white sauce, which is a must with this recipe. Add a few tablespoons of flour to the pan drippings. Stir it in carefully until well dissolved. Now start to make the gravy by adding milk little by little, stirring the entire time to avoid lumping. This takes some patience. When your gravy has reached the required thickness, let it simmer for a while to get the full flavor.

All you need to make this farmhouse dinner ready to serve is a bowl full of mashed potatoes that you have made while the chicken was cooking and, of course, your favorite vegetables.

Grandmothers are supposed to be loving, warm, and kind, and nobody was a better grandmother than Esther. She grew up in the high Idaho desert. The land was dry, the winters were heavy, and the work was hard. When she was small, her family had to carry their drinking water by wagon 20 miles across the sagebrush desert each week. As she raised her family, her husband Wayne had hired-hands, sometimes ten of them, in the fields much of the summer. Every day at noon, Esther fed those hungry men a big meal they called "dinner."

With no central heating in their farm house, she was up at 5:30 each morning to heat the house, stoke the wood stove, and warm the coffee. Following a several course breakfast, she and her daughters started the noon meal. "Dinner" was hearty with meat, potatoes, and gravy, followed by a dessert, pies or cakes. I so admire Esther and women like her. To them, the kitchen was home, and their food was filling and satisfying, enough to keep her men going all day, milking the cows, pitching the hay, and harvesting the potatoes. It wasn't an easy life for anyone, but such women gave it a glamour of its own.

By the time I met Grandma, life of course had become easier. She made adjustment to my new American home smooth and comfortable. With grace and warmth she prepared lovely dishes to greet us when we visited from the nearby college we attended.

And what a dancer Wayne was! Before computers, TV, and the radio, social life in the country centered around Saturday night dances, and that's how they grew up. When the children were born, Esther and Wayne bundled them up and took them along to the dance. On our honeymoon, we by chance met Esther and Wayne in the same Rocky Mountain restaurant, and they invited us to the dance that evening. Grandpa Wayne waltzed me around the floor until my head spun.

Esther and Wayne

Greek Lemon Chicken

from Olga's kitchen, Greece

Servings: 5

This savory chicken main course brings the Mediterranean to your dining table. It is a real favorite in my family. I learned it from Olga during a visit to their home in Sparta, Greece.

Olga

- 1 Whole Chicken
- 2 lbs Potatoes
- 4 Lemons
- Oregano
- ½ - 1 cup Olive oil
- Salt and Pepper

Squeeze the lemons. Peel and slice the potatoes into large pieces. Put the chicken into an oven dish, breast down, and surround with potatoes. Now pour the olive oil over the top of the chicken and into the pan (I use between ½ cup and 1 cup, depending on the pan), add the lemon juice, and put enough hot water to cover the potatoes halfway. Sprinkle the oregano over the potatoes only. Salt and pepper everything well.

Bake at 400 F. for 1 ½ hours. After 50 minutes, turn everything over to bake and brown the other sides of the chicken and potatoes. (If not in a hurry, switch off oven just before done, and with declining heat it will absorb water and juice.)

P.S. Our daughter, Kaarina, places quartered lemons inside the chicken and finds it's even tastier.

Gene prepares his prize-winning olive oil

Olga was a world known classical archeologist at the University of Athens and lectured regularly at Oxford, Cambridge, and many Ivy League universities in the US. She was outspoken, her humor was sharp, and she was always fun to be around. More than once she took us to ancient Greek sites with a narrative and tour that we never forgot.

Olga's husband, Gene, was an economist who worked over thirty years for the American Embassy in Athens where we met him. On the side, Gene owned olive groves on the hills of Mistras, an old Byzantine city high above ancient Sparta. A blend of 10 different olive varieties, Gene's oil was of superb quality and finest flavor – the best we have had anywhere in the Mediterranean, and over the years we have tasted a lot of olive oils. One day, Gene put an ad on the internet saying he had Greek olive oil to send abroad. He was soon shipping crates of oil to New York and other spots in the U.S. where it sold at a premium.

One Saturday afternoon in the early Spring, we drove from Athens to Mistras where Gene demonstrated his trees and production process. Afterwards, he lit the fireplace in a processing shed among the groves, and offered us barbecued sausages. We dipped chunks of country-style heavy white bread in a saucer of his rich green oil and enjoyed the full, complimentary flavors. Even a simple combination of ingredients – if they are the best – can offer an unforgettable culinary experience.

Mistras, on whose misty slopes Gene's olive groves flourish

Pork Chops in Mustard

from Maija's kitchen, Austria

Servings: 4

Treat yourself to these sumptuous chops. They melt in your mouth. You won't regret it.

Maija

- 4 Pork Chops with bone in
- 2 cups Breadcrumbs
- Mustard
- 2-4 tsp Curry Powder
- Salt and Pepper
- 2 Eggs
- Oil and Butter for frying

Be sure your pork chops are not too thick and have some fat on the edges to ensure tenderness. You will need enough breadcrumbs to coat the number of pork chops you are cooking. Have a low wide dish ready for the crumbs to make it easier for coating. Add salt and pepper and curry powder to the crumbs.

Break your eggs into another low wide dish and whip to mix whites and yolks. Spread pork chops evenly with mustard on both sides and then dip them into the egg mixture. Next coat them with crumbs. Have your pan ready to go, either an electric frying pan or your heavy skillet, with butter and corn oil already sizzling (electric pan temperature 350 F, ordinary pan medium-high).

Fry the chops on both sides until they have a beautiful golden color, and then lower the temperature (electric: 250 F; ordinary pan: low) and cover. Simmer for a while until your meat comes soft and tender. Again, if necessary, add some extra oil or butter. The chops should be ready in 20 – 30 minutes time. Serving suggestion: applesauce goes well with your chops as a side dish as does German red cabbage salad, and sauerkraut.

     Maija and I became friends when I was still young. Maija was living at home with her family in Finland when I was a student in her hometown. Years later, when Michael and I were at our first posting in Milan, Italy, Maija had married an Austrian husband and had two sons in Lienz, Austria, high in the Alps near the Austro-Italian boarder. We had a chance to visit them a few times and to enjoy Maija's good home cooking, including these delicious pork chops.

     Having a young family with four children under five was a challenge when we arrived at our first State Department posting in Milan, Italy. Our car was stolen the first week after it arrived. It took a month to replace it, and in the meantime we were all on public transportation in a strange new city. We had three car accidents, one of which was when a group of Mafioso crashed into us, or that is what our insurance company wrote when it said it had decided to pay our claim without waiting for a settlement from the other party. Our hyperactive two year old was in the emergency room three times. And finally a transformer in our apartment exploded and caught the storage room on fire. Our two year old came running to me to say the house is on fire! I saw the smoke and believed him.

     The day after the fire, the Consul General called Mike into his office to say that he had decided to send him on an official visit to the Merano, a beautiful city in the Italian Alps. There were two conditions, however: He had to take me along with him, at his expense and without the children; and after interviewing community leaders, he had to do a report on political and economic trends he found in the city. Merano was in South Tyrol, and was a place where mornings people could ski in the mountains above, and in the afternoons walk down its quiet paths lined with palm and peach trees. To me it was therapy – and I've always been grateful to that man for realizing what I was going through.

     Maija took our three older children, and the youngest one remained with friends in Milan, while Michael worked with his interviews, and I had a lovely few days winding down in Merano. Just as with so many food dishes, it took the bitter to know the sweet.

Roast Loin of Pork with Prunes

Servings: 10

from Ian's kitchen, Italy

Ian served this dish one evening in the fall when the weather was cold and rainy. Our residence, Villa Laura, was filled with wonderful aromas when the staff from Michael's office arrived for an office party.

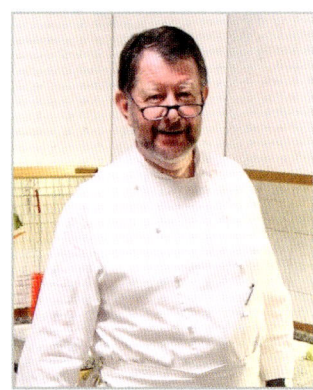

Ian

- 4 lb Loin of Pork, boneless and de-skinned
- 2 Garlic Cloves, crushed
- ½ White Onion, finely chopped
- ½ cup Chopped Parsley
- 20 Black Prunes without stones
- Olive Oil
- 4 Tbs Butter, cold
- Black Pepper and Salt
- String (kitchen twine) and tin foil

Trim the loan pork and cut the center of the pork open by making a slit into the center along the length of the loin. Salt and pepper.

Mince 10 prunes, onions, parsley, and garlic. Season with salt and pepper. Chop the cold butter into small pieces and add to the mixture. Place the mixture along the center of the pork, and on top of it set the remaining whole prunes in a row. Roll up the loin of pork and tie with the string. Place a small part of tin foil over each end of the pork to stop the stuffing from escaping. Place the pork onto an oiled roasting tray (with the cut upwards), then season again with salt and pepper.

Roast in a pre-heated oven at 500 F for 20 minutes. This will seal the pork. Continue to roast at 275 F until cooked. It is important to turn the pork only one time.

Suggestion: You might serve this main course accompanied with Savory Potatoes (recipe in *The Nomad Chef*), glazed apples, and a port wine sauce.

This recipe is from Ian, the chef for our American ambassador in Rome. Ian was from Scotland and was married to an Italian wife. He occasionally worked in my kitchen at Villa Laura when I needed extra help or he was free. It was always a joy to be with Ian. I liked working alongside this talented cook and learned much from him. I also shared in his philosophy. Ian once wrote to me:

"In the kitchen you should start each morning with nil in your fridge or freezer and the very best food that you can afford. In life one should just work, play and rest hard; have all the fun that you can each day. Eat and drink only the best. To teach one person one new thing each day of my life makes me go to bed a very happy man." - Ian

Salmon Baked in Cream

Servings: 4-5

from Ulla's kitchen, Finland

My friend Ulla's variation on baked salmon adds a sumptuous flavor to an old favorite. This main course is fast and simple, and excellent for any dinner party.

Ulla

- 2 lbs Salmon (filleted)
- Lemon Pepper
- Sea Salt
- 1 ½ cups Cream
- ½ cup Cognac or Brandy
- Fresh Dill

Bake your salmon seasoned slightly with lemon pepper and sea salt in your oven at 350 F.

While the salmon is baking, whip the cream until half-whipped. Then mix the cognac into the cream. After the salmon has baked 20 minutes, remove it from the oven and pour entire mixture over the salmon.

Return the salmon to the oven and bake for an additional 20 minutes. After baking, garnish with fresh dill.

    Ulla was one of my closest Finnish friends, a real lady, and an ideal hostess. Her husband, Make, wrote a travel magazine, and in the course of his work they traveled and ate at some of the world's finest hotels and restaurants.

    Ulla knew what good food was and how to make it for her own guests. How many times over the years have we had refined dinners sitting at Ulla's immaculately set table, across from Finnish actresses, industrialists, and their many other friends! And we have enjoyed wonderful moments together around tables from Helsinki, to the Arctic Circle, to Rome, and to Boston and Washington.

    Yet, as this recipe shows, the best dishes often are simple and hardly complicated.

Tenderloin Fillet

Servings: 4

from Nellie's kitchen, South Africa

This recipe is from my South African friend and neighbor Nellie, who with her sister-in-law catered several dinners and evening events at our home. Her dishes were always unbelievably well done, as you will see from this fillet.

Meat
2 lb Tenderloin Fillet

½ cup Oil

   Mustard

   Garlic

   Black peppercorns, crushed

1 Tb Butter

1 Bouillon cube

Sauce
½ cup Brandy

½ cup Red Wine

1 tsp Mustard Powder

½ tsp Garlic Powder

3/4 – 1 cup Cream

2 tsp Corn Starch or regular Flour

Nellie

Rub the entire fillet with oil, fine mustard and garlic. Roll it then in fine black peppercorns. Warm 1/2 cup oil, butter, and the bouillon cube in a pan until it is dissolved. Now add the tenderloin and fry it until it is nicely browned and until the meat thermometer reaches 150 F (medium rare), or slightly higher if you prefer more done. Cut the meat into fairly thick slices and leave for 1-2 hours to stand and cool.

Ten minutes before serving, pour brandy onto the fillet and drippings. Flame the brandy carefully, making certain nothing flammable is near the pan and that the stove fan is turned to high. The fillet pieces will flame for several seconds. Once the flame dies, remove the meat from the pan immediately and let rest.

Now make your sauce: Pour the wine, mustard powder, and garlic into the saucepan with drippings and cook until only half of the liquid is left. Add the cream and cook for 2 minutes. If necessary, thicken the gravy with 2 tsp of corn starch or ordinary flour. Pour the gravy over the meat and serve.

    Nellie and her husband, Hermann, lived in a picture-book two-story thatched roof home next to us in Pretoria. A high brick wall separated our homes. In October, South Africa's springtime, the Jacaranda trees lining streets in front of our houses turned deep violet, an inverse of colors that made the entire city turn from green to purple.

    Still today I can hear Nellie's joyful laugh sifting over the wall from her yard to ours. If the African warm sun didn't cheer me up, her merriment did. Nellie's catering business often came very handy for me. When I didn't have time to do representational cooking, I hired Nellie.

    South African cooking is a fusion of many nationalities: Dutch, Indian, British, African, American – pretty international. This was how Nellie's cooking was. One evening we were invited for dinner in her beautiful home, and this meat dish was the main course on the menu. A large marble counter table was covered with 30-40 candles, and in their light and with classical music as background, we enjoyed an unforgettable evening.

Turkey Roast with Orange Sauce
from Katerina's kitchen, Greece

Servings: 4-5

Katerina served this turkey roast one evening in her artistic Athens residence. It is another of those recipes that is simple to make and refined to serve. Surround it with Savory Potatoes, and French Baby Peas, and you have an enjoyable feast for your guests. The recipes for both the potatoes and peas are found in The Nomad Chef.

Katerina

- 3 lb Turkey Breast or Turkey Roast
- 2 Oranges
- Dijon Mustard
- Salt
- Pepper
- ¼ cup White Wine
- ¼ cup Olive Oil

Place the turkey breast up inside a roast pan and spread a layer of Dijon mustard on top the roast. Take juice from the 2 oranges and pour slowly over the turkey, and then slowly pour the olive oil over the turkey, leaving both the excess oil and orange juice in the bottom of the pan. Salt and pepper. Now pour the white wine into the bottom of the roast pan.

Bake at 350 F for about 1 ½ hours or until the meat reaches a temperature of about 170 F. Baste continually with the oil-juice-wine mixture from the bottom of the pan.

    Katerina and her husband Dimitris were dear friends who lived not far from us in Athens. Katerina was an actress and a lawyer. She also worked on the city council of her municipality. Dimitris was a TV and movie director. Her brother Spiros, a retired scientist and Greek-American pharmaceutical executive, lived with them. They were fun, colorful, generous and interesting. I enjoyed immensely Katerina and her family.

    It was especially hard to beat their annual costume party held at Carnival time in Greece. People arrived at their home in spectacular costumes, some of which came from the wardrobe of the Athens Theater. The evening picked up and ran into the wee hours when Katerina's and Dimitris' son, Paris, DJ'ed some great dance music. But best of all about Katerina were the meals she served and the hospitality she offered. This dish was only one of the many that we enjoyed as pampered guests.

Vitello Tonnato *("Tuna'ed Veal")*
from Signor and Signora Riva's kitchen, Italy

Servings: 10

I acquired this exceptional summer dish recipe during our first diplomatic assignment in Milan, Italy. It is simply perfect on a warm summer afternoon - delicious, light, colorful, and cool. It was a favorite among the Milanese, and definitely one of my favorites, too.

- 3 lbs Veal Roast (leg or loin)
- 3 Carrots
- ½ tsp Salt
- 3 cans Tuna
- 3 Medium Onions
- 4 Celery Stocks
- 1/8 tsp Pepper
- ½ cup Pickled Peppers
  - Capers and Pickled Vegetables
  - Mayonnaise

Combine the veal, carrots, onion, celery, and salt in a pan. Add water to cover the meat and bring to a boil. Reduce the heat and cover tightly. Simmer, turning once, until the veal is done (temperature about 150 F), about one hour. Move to a platter and let cool. Save the broth.* Wrap the meat and place it in the refrigerator until well chilled. Then slice the veal into thin slices, 1/8 – 1/4 inch thick. Spread the slices neatly on a serving platter.

Drain the tuna and then put it through a food processor or hand grinder to make it into a puree. Add only enough broth to make a thin tuna paste. (If grinding by hand, you may want to add some liquid to help the tuna move through the grinder.) Add sufficient mayonnaise to make a nice consistency.

Cover the veal slices with a layer of tuna sauce. Top the tuna with capers and surround the veal with pickled peppers and vegetables. Once the tuna sauce is on top the veal, you must serve it within a couple of hours. Otherwise it will start to lose its texture. However, you can make the tuna sauce a day before if you keep it covered and refrigerated. Spread it on the veal before serving. Serve cold.

* The remaining broth makes a base for a perfect Risotto. See the recipe for Risotto Milanese, elsewhere in *The Nomad Chef*

    Not long after our young family arrived in Milan on our first tour abroad, I told the Riva's, our retired and very traditional Italian neighbors, that I would like to learn a typical Italian dish. Coming from me, the spouse of an American diplomat, this was a serious matter. They told me they were delighted to help, but, they added quickly that it was "...too much to leave to the woman of the house." So, it was Signor Riva who came over to teach me how to prepare one of their favorite dishes and the risotto that went with it. As I followed his careful instructions, his wife kept a vigilant eye through her kitchen window into ours, to make sure her husband paid attention only to the cooking, which he did!

    The result was this magnificent combination: a Risotto Milanese for the opener and Vitello Tonnato for the main course – as they do it in Italy, in Lombardy. I'm absolutely certain that Signora Riva would have been as good if not better instructor. But I was double lucky – I learned to do two fantastic dishes – and I got a glimpse into an old Italian culture that has probably faded by now, at least in cosmopolitan Milan.

Carrot Soup

from Ian's kitchen, Italy

Servings: 4

What a refreshing opener for any summer or winter meal. So refined; so healthy!

Ian

- 1 lb Carrots
- 1-2 cups fresh Chicken Stock preferably home-made
- 1 Tb Butter
  - Cilantro
  - Fresh Thyme (a pinch)
  - Black Pepper
- ½ Lemon

Peel the carrots and chop them into small pieces. Cook them in enough water to cover, adding more liquid, if needed, until soft. After cooking, let them cool. Add the butter.

Next, blend your cooked carrots in a blender and then pour them into a soup pan. You should add just enough chicken stock to thin the puree and add flavor. Bring to a hot temperature, but don't boil. Sprinkle your soup with fresh thyme and black pepper. If your stock was already salty, additional salt may not be necessary. Taste to determine. Squeeze in half a lemon. Again, correct the seasoning if necessary. Finish by sprinkling with cilantro just before serving. Serve warm before your pasta or main course and salad.

P.S. When I cook vegetables, I save the liquid and freeze it to defrost when I am ready to make soups. It makes a good soup base. Also, you can make this soup even more tasty by preparing your own chicken stock.

This carrot soup came from Ian, the chef on the staff of our American Ambassador in Rome. It perfectly fit the setting when Ian served it on the roof terrace of the Ambassador's Residence that overlooked the ancient Roman wall. An ornate stone gate, commanding during the day and illuminated at night, opened through the massive wall. I really can't express the magic of such an evening event.

As we dined we could see the Appian Way as it passed through on its journey to and from from southern Italy and Greece beyond there. Travelers dating back to the time Christ had entered the "eternal city" through this gate, surely Saint Peter and Saint Paul among them. The Appian Way continued only a short distance farther before opening into the great Colosseum and Roman Forum. The old pavement stones still lined the way, stop points where perhaps someone important had lingered, or miracles took place.

That evening we sat there, pondering the saints and sinners who had marched along the road before us, as we enjoyed Ian's Carrot Soup. (More recipes from Ian elsewhere in *The Nomad Chef*.)

Rome's ancient Colosseum, where the Appian Way reached its destination

Crab Salad

Servings: 8

from the kitchen of the Golden Fox, Greece

It is not easy to describe how much pleasure I get spending a warm slow afternoon while gazing down onto a breathtaking seascape, with a delicately prepared fresh seafood on the table before me. That is how I first experienced this wonderful crab salad, high above the Adriatic island of Corfu. But this salad is refreshingly tasty any afternoon, anywhere.

Nikos

- 1 cup Mayonnaise
- ¼ cup Light Cream
- 5-6 oz Frozen Mixed Vegetables
- 1 lb Crab (or Imitation Crab, Mussels, or an equal amounts of all)
- 1 tsp Mustard Powder
- Salt and pepper

Mix the mayonnaise, mustard, and cream and refrigerate for at least four hours. Put the frozen vegetables into very hot water for ten minutes, but do not cook. Drain off the water well.

Chop the crab into small pieces.

Mix all the ingredients together, and serve.

What pleasure I find from a warm afternoon, a beautiful world around me, good friends, and delicious dishes

    This recipe is from Nikos, chef at The Golden Fox on the Greek island of Corfu. Corfu is a verdant and majestic island that has always inspired artists and writers. Henry Miller visited Corfu to write "The Colossus of Maroussi," Gerald Durrell's "My Family and other Animals" takes place in Corfu, and the James Bond film, "For your Eyes Only," starts here.

    Of course it also attracted us. One warm summer morning in the hot month of August we drove through the hill village of Lakones, 900 feet above the old port of Paleokastritsa. The view was breathtaking. You felt that you were halfway between earth and heaven. Thirsty and looking for a place to enjoy the view for a little while longer, we stopped at The Golden Fox hotel and were greeted warmly by the Michalos family, its owners.

    This was a small hotel with only 15 rooms, a coffee bar, a gift shop with local handcrafts, and a restaurant. Michael and I ended up sitting on the terrace admiring the view, sipping refreshing juices, and getting acquainted with our new friends. As is so common in Greece, it was a family business that employed parents, children, their spouses, and now grandchildren. They all

Nikos's Crab Salad could not have been more perfect on the table before us, overlooking the Adriatic below

worked together. A teenage granddaughter ran the pool bar by herself without salary or complaint. She told me that at summer's end, when she was ready to go for a school trip outside Greece, she received generous pocket money and her air travel. Everyone's efforts supported the family business.

Nikos, their chef, was married to Katerina Michalos whose Greek grandfather had worked as a chef in Switzerland before returning to his home country to open a restaurant in Paleokastritsa, on the west side of Corfu. There, his daughter (and Katerina's mother), Roula, met a young man who had a bakery in Paleokastritsa, and when Roula married him, her father taught his new son-in-law to be an outstanding chef. The Golden Fox was born, and years later, when Katerina married Nikos, her father took Nikos in the same way into his kitchen to pass recipes and skills.

Over the years we have returned to the Golden Fox more than once to enjoy its fresh air, awesome views, and many delicious meals.

Cream of Apple Soup

Servings: 12

from Leon's kitchen, Greece

Soups are excellent first dishes and I have served them often. In the best recipes, such as this one, they nicely blend the soup's folk kitchen tradition with a gourmet mood. Everyone is happy with a good soup.

Leon

- 2 lbs Onions, sliced
- 4 Apples, sliced
- 3 Potatoes, sliced or cubed
- 6 oz Crème Fraiche
- 3 Egg yolks
- 1 qt Chicken Stock, (or 3 Chicken Bouillon cubes and water)
- Salt
- Pepper
- 1 tsp Curry Powder
- 2 Tbs Olive Oil or Corn Oil

In a large soup pan sauté the onions. Add the apples, curry powder and chicken stock. Bring the soup base to a boil, and then lower the heat and simmer the soup about 45 minutes or until the ingredients are done.

Now put most of the soup into the blender, leaving some of it in the pot in order to give the soup some chunky texture. Blend the portion in the blender, and put it back into the pot with the remaining soup. Add the crème fraiche and egg yolks, one at a time, whipping the entire time. Heat up the soup slowly. Check the seasoning to taste. Serve and enjoy.

      This is a recipe from one of our Athens chefs, Leon, a Cypriot Greek. There is a Cypriot Greek proverb which goes like this: "He, who is unhappy in the morning, is unhappy all day." This was certainly not true about Leon. He was always happy, smiling, and full of energy. This happy spirit flowed throughout his kitchen. When I met him for the first time, he greeted me with his arms full of beautiful red roses. And when he served a soup like this one, it was as good as the roses.

      I made Cream of Apple Soup often for representational dinners, especially in the fall. On one occasion in Virginia, my husband was organizing and hosting a conference for people from Europe and the United States. Since it was autumn, I thought at least one of the conference luncheon's dishes served should be seasonal. So I took this recipe to the convention center and asked if they would prepare it as the opener, and they agreed.

      On the day of the luncheon I was anxious to see how people liked my soup. Actually, I think I was starting to get a little nervous as I looked across the table toward our city's mayor who was next to my husband. Finally, she interrupted their conversation to dip her spoon into the soup. She took a taste, looked up, and exclaimed, "This is delicious!" In fact, people enjoyed it very much. By the end of the luncheon I had heard many thanks for this fine Cream of Apple Soup that Leon taught me.

Perhaps because autumn is harvest time, it has so many dishes associated with it. I always seek fall recipes for family and friends during these three months when summer changes to winter.

Eggplant Salad

from Kamala's kitchen, Sri Lanka

Servings: 6

This salad, with its vibrant Asian presence, is from Sri Lanka, a beautiful country resting off the east coast of India. You will love its exotic blends of tasty spices and vegetables.

Kamala

Canola Oil* for frying

- 1 Eggplant (long and thin), cut into thin strips
- 1 Bitter Gourd, thinly sliced (optional)
- ½ Red Onion, sliced
- ½ Tomato, sliced
- 1 Tb Lemon or Lime Juice
-   Salt
-   Pepper
- 1 Tb Sugar
- 1 tsp Turmeric
- ½ tsp Dijon Mustard

*or Olive Oil for high temperatures

Begin by mixing about 1/2 tsp salt and turmeric with a little water in a bowl. Dip the sliced eggplant in the bowl to coat it with the turmeric mixture. This will prevent the eggplant from discoloring. Set aside

Pour the canola oil into a small deep pan, preferably iron, about 2-3 inches deep. Heat the oil to high and fry the eggplant and bitter gourd slices quickly until it has a bit of color. Drain well. (Bitter gourd when in season can be found at Asian stores and some supermarkets. You can exclude it if not available.) If I am not in a hurry I place the fried vegetables in a colander and let them drain for several hours. Otherwise I just put them on a plate lined with a paper towel with another paper towel on top to drain the excess oil.

Make the sauce by adding lemon, salt, pepper, sugar, turmeric and Dijon mustard. Place your drained eggplant (and gourd) into a serving dish and pour the sauce over them. Decorate with chopped onions and tomatoes.

This is a recipe from Kamala who with her husband, Neville, were our neighbors and friends in Chancellorsville, a now quiet Virginia countryside where a great Civil War battle was once fought. They were originally from Sri Lanka, and their family was dedicated to medicine. Neville was an anesthesiologist, Kamala had worked as a physician's assistant. Their two daughters were physicians, and their husbands were also medical doctors. (You will find a nutritious recipe from one of Kamala's daughters, Nimali, elsewhere in *The Nomad Chef*: "Strawberry Salsa.")

In addition to being an outstanding cook, Kamala was a rare asset to our entire community, knitting our neighborhood together amidst the spreading woods that separated our homes and lives. She invited us to take walks with her in the mornings, gathering us to chat when we met on the streets. In what I'm sure was a fine Sri Lankan tradition, Kamala and her husband loved get-togethers and parties.

Best of all, Kamala shared with us her wonderful cooking, with its rich spicy Sri Lankan aromas and flavors. We enjoyed many lovely meals in her home. I have more than one of her recipes on *The Nomad Chef*.

Kamala and Neville

Esau's Red Lentil Soup

Servings: 6

from Mary's kitchen, Maryland

Here is a warm and tasty soup that is especially good in the fall and winter. I have served it both as an opener for formal representational events and as a evening meal at home. Esau's timeless soup comes from Biblical Middle Eastern tradition, so this recipe with bacon has to be a somewhat gentile version. I love all kinds of soups and as a matter of fact could eat them at every meal every day. Throwing ingredients into a pot is fun. While doing so I listen to an audiobook, and the time slips by quickly as I made something special for family or friends.

- 2 slices Bacon
- 1 Medium Onion, chopped
- 1 Minced Garlic Clove
- 1 Tb Parsley, chopped
- 1 Medium Tomato, diced
- 1 sliced Carrot
- 1 Stalk Celery, chopped
- ¼ tsp Oregano
- 1/2 tsp Cumin
- 1/2 tsp Tumeric
- 1 cup Red Lentils
- ½ cup Tomato Juice
- 3 ½ cups Beef Stock
- 1 Tb Lemon Juice

Cut your bacon into smaller slices and then sauté them in a large saucepan for a few minutes until they release some drippings. Then add onion, garlic, parsley, tomato, carrot, celery, and oregano. Sauté until the onion is transparent. Add the lentils and remaining ingredients. Bring to a boil, reduce the heat, and simmer until the lentils and vegetables are tender, about 30 minutes. Puree' 2 cups of the soup in a blender. Return to soup and combine. Add lemon juice.

Add salt and pepper to taste. Adjust the seasoning. Garnish with chopped parsley and/or chopped hard-boiled eggs. Add liquid as necessary to achieve the desired thickness. Serve warm.

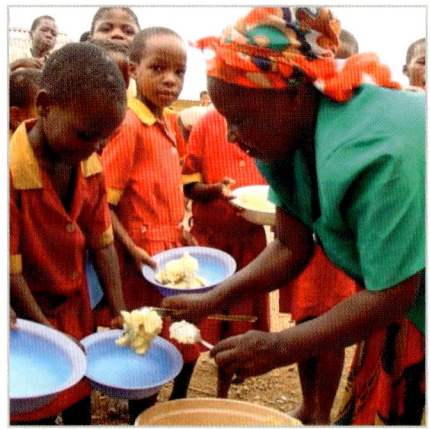

My husband Michael's first job out of university was working as an economist at the US Department of Agriculture's Foreign Agricultural Service. One autumn evening, his boss and his wife, Mary, invited us to their home for dinner. We started with Esau's Red Lentil Soup. My culinary journey was still in its early stages, and that evening I learned how a little thought can transform even an informal get together into a memorable dinner event. The lentil soup was such an appetizing and appropriate choice for the fall time of year. The smoky flavor of the bacon and extra fullness it brought, offset the nippy weather, outside that night. Unfortunately, I lost track of Mary decades ago, but her recipe has lived on in my kitchen since that pleasant night in her home.

Over the years, Michael worked often on food issues. At the end of his career, he was the Deputy American Representative to the two UN organizations that dealt with food and agriculture: the World Food Program and the Food and Agriculture Organization

I once accompanied Mike as he traveled to Swaziland to observe the distribution of American food aid to some of the world's most hungry people. As I taught some of the children games we played when I was small, I was humbled as I saw how much the food assistance meant to them. I also saw once again how even in the poorest of circumstances, a good meal is a joyous moment for everyone involved.

It was also a delight for me to see how American food aid made possible school lunch programs for children who otherwise would have never known a full stomach. The corn, ground into an enriched pap, might not seem gourmet to everyone, but for them the school lunch was a feast. The smiles on their small faces told the entire story.

Insalata Romana

from Ian's kitchen, Italy

Servings: 4 - 6 servings

Arugula and parmesan cheese salad is often served in Italian restaurants, but I doubt you have had this version before. This salad is simple and full of flavor -- especially on warm summer days when you don't feel like eating a lot, and your body requires extra salt. The recipe is unique in calling for the prosciutto to be fried. The frying process gives the salad its character.

Ian

- 8 oz Arugula Lettuce
- 4 oz Parma Ham (prosciutto)
- 4 oz Italian Parmesan Cheese, fresh and preferably whole, unshredded
- 1 Tb Olive Oil

Separate the ham pieces carefully without breaking them. Cut them into small pieces with kitchen scissors, about 1-inch in length and then sauté in a large frying pan that has about 1 tablespoon of olive oil until they are crispy (or, alternatively, bake them in the oven at 400 F for 10 minutes on each side). It is important not to burn the ham, but make sure it becomes crispy.

Wash and dry the arugula salad leaves and place in a large bowl. Mix the ham with the leaves.

Take a cheese cutter and shave your Parmesan cheese into flat thin slices and fold them into the salad bowl, leaving a few on top as decoration. If you serve it on individual dishes, lay the cheese on the top of the lettuce mixture.

The salad is good to eat as it is or you can use your favorite Italian oil and vinegar as dressing. Balsamic vinegar blends very well with the cheese and arugula.

The Nomad Chef

One day soon after we moved to Rome I went to pick up Greek visitors from Fiumicino airport and got lost on my way home. I have to say that Rome's winding roads and one-way streets give a Roman meaning to the Greek word "chaos!" When we finally arrived at Villa Laura all exhausted, Ian who was working for us that day had this wonderful salad waiting. Placed around the salad was fresh Italian bread, perfect for hungry and frustrated travelers.

One of the secrets to this recipe is the Parmesan cheese. Even in Italy, there is nothing like real Parmesan cheese (*parmigiano reggiano*) or Parma ham (*prosciutto di Parma*) from central Italy's Emilia Romagna region. Some neighboring provinces also make a similar cheese (*grana padano*) that is very good. In taste, it is not quite as colorful in flavor as *parmigiano reggiano*, but it sells for less in Italian markets. Parmesan cheese from anywhere else lacks the rich, full flavor of the real thing.

There are many kinds of prosciutto on store shelves, but none of it compares to Parma ham. Never cooked and cured over long periods of time from pork fed in Emilia Romagna, the ham is served in thinly shaved slices and is normally eaten uncooked. Its flavor is so full that you need no more than 2-3 of these thin slices to satisfy your pallet.

When I got home with my guests, we enjoyed Ian's salad from the terrace of our Trastevere Villa Laura. Its view across Renaissance Rome made every dish all the better.

Mediterranean Soup
from Marja's kitchen, Finland

Servings: 4-6

I don't like soups, I love them. Soups and stews are comfort foods that bring warmth to our bodies whatever is happening outside. Marja's Mediterranean Soup carries a taste of the sea to your table. The recipe doesn't involve working endless hours in the kitchen. It entails more shopping than chopping. You don't need to have homemade stock for it. It will still taste good from store bought fish or chicken broths, or even from clam juice, or a mixture of these. You can be creative. The key to good stew is in the seasoning, and that's especially true with this soup. It is quite fast to make because you don't cook fish long, 10-15 minutes at the most for the thickest fillets.

Marja and her husband, Jaakko

Fish Stock
2 qts Fish stock

1 Leek, coarsely chopped

1 Onion, coarsely chopped

1 Celery stalk, coarsely chopped

4-5 Bay leaves

some parsley stalks

a few black peppercorns

½ cup White Cooking Wine

Salt and White Pepper

Soup
½ lbs Trout or salmon

½ cup Almond flour

Place the fish stock ingredients in a large pan or pot and bring to just under a boil (the slower you do this the more flavor the finished stock will have). Skim, turn down the heat to simmer for 20 minutes, skimming again if necessary. (If you are making stock from scratch place the bones into the pot along with the rest of the stock ingredients and add water enough to cover them by about two fingers, depending on how strong you want the stock to be. The less water, the richer it will be.)

Turn off the heat and let the stock settle, then pour it through a fine sieve. Return the stock to the pot and add the fish which has been cut into smallish pieces. Simmer them about 10-15 minutes.

Add almond flour. (If you have thin slivered almonds you can also crush them in your hand and sprinkle them also into the soup.)

- ½ - 1 cup Half and Half
- 1/3 cup Mascarpone cheese
- 8-10 Large frozen shrimp, defrosted
- ¼ cup Teriyaki sauce
- 2 Tbs Lemon juice

Add the half and half and the mascarpone. Stir well and simmer until the cheese is well melted. Now add your shelled and rinsed shrimp. Make sure that you don't bring them to a boil.

Stir in the teriyaki sauce and lemon. Ladle into serving bowls and decorate with fresh dill.

Notes:
If you don't have almond flour in your pantry, simply blanch them and grind almonds in your processor into a fine powder

If you wish to prepare your own fish stock: 1 lb. fish bones, preferably flounder, sole, turbot, or halibut.

Marja and Jaakko were nomads like I am. They were both born in Karelia. Like mine, their parents had to leave their home when the war with Russia began. Our roots grew on the same ground, on Karelian ridges. When we first met at an Embassy party in Helsinki, we immediately recognized that we were from the same tribe.

Both Marja and Jaakko graduated from the Helsinki School of Economics. Jaakko was Marja's soccer team coach—and their five decades of marriage all started there. Jaakko's hobby was shooting and his office was full of trophies won as one of Finland's top marksmen. Marja went into the business world. But she soon found she wasn't happy working in somebody else's firm and started her own design company. Marja had vision, and she wanted to create something beautiful and original for women in Finland. But her clothing, silk, scarves, and ties soon reached far beyond Finland's borders, across China and Korea in a chain bearing her name. This was her "Silk Route." In Finland, a country known for its artistic modern design, Marja's shop and brand "Marja Kurki" was among the best.

We often enjoyed warm sumptuous meals in Marja's modern Helsinki home on one of Helsinki's many islands. Around the table, we supped her Mediterranean soup – inspired by the view from their home overlooking the sea in Spain - together with other friends. Hannu Kiiski, a distinguished professor of cello at Finland's renowned Sibelius Academy's, joined us, his music the nicest appetizer one could wish. When he played the melody to the folk song "The Hills of Karelia," we saw Karelia's hills before us and of course our eyes filled with tears.

A passage in one of Marja Kurki's brochures goes: *"Make the world yours. Blow your mind, do something new. Feel the joy of making things happen. Let your intuition guide you."* Good advice in everything!

Hannu's delightful strains filled Maija's beautiful home

Marja's shop on Helsinki's stylish Esplanaadi square

Parmesan Cheese Boats

Servings 4

from Oscar's kitchen, Athens

This recipe makes a fantastic parmesan boats that you fill with salad leaves to make a tasty and glamorous salad.

4 cups Italian Parmesan Cheese, grated

Green Salad of your choice, preferably Arugula

Oscar

Grate the parmesan cheese or buy ready grated. (Note: use real Italian parmesan to get the true full flavor. You can use *Grana Padano,* which is a little less expensive than the richer flavored *Parmigiano Reggiano*.).

Draw 6-inch circles on parchment baking paper. Fill the circles with a 1-cup layer of the grated cheese. Bake them in the oven at 350 F about 15-17 minutes until they are golden brown. When they are still warm, put the soft parmesan circles carefully around a bowl or a rolling pin to give them the shape of a boat. The way you mold the boat will give it a different shape and character. I have used both. Let them cool for a bit; then loosen carefully. This may take some time unless you have lots of rolling pins!

Fill the boats with your favorite salad. Arugula leaves, for instance, have a flavor that goes especially well with parmesan. Surround the boats with salad leaves on the serving plates, and sprinkle some parmesan slivers over the salad. You can also break the baked parmesan into pieces and put them on top of your prepared salad. Very tasty and attractive.

Oscar, from Sierra Leone, came from a family that had spent most of their lives on the staff of the American Ambassador's residence in Athens. He carried on that family tradition as chef for us when we lived in Athens. Among his specialties were these sophisticated yet quite easy to make Parmesan boats.

I served a salad nicely resting in beautiful parmesan boats at a luncheon in honor of Orthodox Archbishop for North America Demetrios and Archbishop Cristodoulos, the head of the Orthodox Church in Greece. The luncheon was only a few days after the September 11th attacks. Demetrios touched everyone present with his eloquence, warmth, and grace. While we were preparing the meal, Mike left to hear him speak at a memorial event at the University of Athens. Demetrios brought many of the audience to tears as he put the 9/11 tragedy into the context of the Christian virtues needed so badly in the aftermath.

A number of top Greek American leaders from the United States were also present at our luncheon. I spent much of my time lobbying them over lunch to support one of my favorite projects in Athens, a home for street children run by an extraordinary young Orthodox priest. It didn't hurt my lobbying that the luncheon Oscar served, including this Parmesan Boat Salad, was just perfect. I was delighted when some of our guests agreed to visit the project the following day.

On cliffs in central Greece is a chain of monasteries called Meteora which means "suspended in the air." Our friend Father Giannis was then in charge of one of them, Aghia Triada. Once during a visit, he took us into his quarters to share a quick bite to eat. He instantly made us a tasty lunch of Greek salad, cabbage salad, and country bread. Since Father Giannis was nearly blind I joined in to help, but he quickly noticed I wasn't making the salad leaves small enough. "This way," he said, and I learned about Greek salads.

Aghia Triada Monastery

Pasta Salad

from Ken's kitchen, Greece

Servings: 8

This recipe is excellent for buffet luncheons or dinners.

Ken

- 1 lb Pasta Noodles
- 1 cup Artichoke Hearts, halved
- 1 Garlic Clove, chopped
- 1 can Tuna
- 1 cup Sun-dried Tomatoes
- 1 Pepper, green or red, sliced thinly
- ¼ cup Olive Oil
- 1 Tb Capers
- A few Kalamata Olives (optional)

Cook the pasta (rigatoni, penne, or shells for 4-6 people) according to package directions. Add the artichokes, garlic, and tuna. If you use tuna in oil, you can use some of the oil if you wish. Otherwise, drain the tuna before adding.

Mix in the sun dried tomatoes cut into small pieces. Add the pepper, cut into small slices, the capers, and olive oil to taste.

You can add a few Kalamata olives for extra color and taste.

    I believe that anyone can be successful in the kitchen if they have confidence and a desire to work at it. After all, we all have thousands of years of cookery in our blood. The passion of an excellent chef, however, is like the passion of an artist.

    Ken, who worked for the American ambassador in Athens, was one of these chefs. He came from Canada to work in Athens. It was easy for him to be like Greeks, obsessed with the sea. Ken bought an apartment with a view of the Aegean, and this way he relaxed after his hectic hours in the ambassador's kitchen.

    Athens was a night city where evening dinner parties were popular. Having an outstanding kitchen was a must. Ken gave the American Embassy Residence a reputation for serving fantastic meals, whether you went to an event for 150 or for 6 people. He was generous enough to give me a few of his recipes, and this is one of them.

"Reindeer" Salad with Grapefruit

Servings: 4

from the kitchen of Reader's Digest Finland

This salad is simple, easy, and exotic, especially if you manage to get smoked reindeer. Of course, reindeer meat is not easily available outside of Scandinavia, so use any other thinly sliced or chopped meat, especially smoked. Italian prosciutto works well as does smoked chopped turkey, pastrami, and chipped beef.

- 8 slices Smoked Reindeer, sliced extra thin, or other thinly sliced meat
- 8 wedges Canned Grapefruit (or fresh pink grapefruit)
- Lettuce leaves
- Olive Oil

First, arrange the salad leaves attractively on the plates. Alternate reindeer and grapefruit slices.

Add some olive oil over your salad, if you like.

We had this fresh inviting opener at a lunch as guests of Readers Digest's Finnish offices. Such an unusual combination – you wouldn't guess that it fits together so well. Of course, in Finland reindeer is a domestic animal that ranges free during parts of the year in Lapland, that vast wilderness in the northern regions of Scandinavia.

Once when we were based at the Embassy in Helsinki, my husband arranged a trip for the American ambassador, Keith Nyborg, to Lapland in order to meet with the Sami tribe leaders (you will find recipes from Keith's wife, Raija, elsewhere in *The Nomad Chef*). This might have been one of the first visits by an American ambassador to the Sami people. Keith spoke Finnish, and easily carried on conversations with everyone we met. As the big black Cadillac wound its way north across the snowy tundra, the telephone lines were buzzing as one Sami family after another phoned their friends to tell that the ambassador was now passing their home.

When we finally arrived, Lappish herders were doing the annual round-up where they gathered reindeer from winter grazing. Keith had grown up on a ranch, and he was still running it when President Reagan appointed him ambassador to Finland. As he watched our hosts rope the reindeer, he asked if he could try.

To their total amazement Keith whipped a lasso across the pen and caught a reindeer by the right front leg on his first try. This wasn't easy, but just as it was supposed to be done. To the Sami people it was the sign of a master roper. The air erupted in a big Lappish equivalent of Hurrah! The head of the Sami association believed Keith's lasso had some magical powers and followed him around for some time. Keith finally gave his lasso as a gift, and the Sami leader gave Keith his. Keith later told us, "All I can say is that the Lord truly blessed me that day. I am not that good a roper."

America's reputation flew high in Lapland that snowy spring day. Sometime later, the Sami's presented Keith a tapestry with an "earmark" embroidered onto it. They told him the earmark was officially registered in his name. They added that there were only two non-Sami's who had earmarks registered in their names. Keith was one of them, and the President of Finland was the other.

Amb. Keith and Raija Nyborg with the head of the Sami Association.

Tuna Salad
from Luana's kitchen, Italy

Servings: 4

This everyday Italian salad makes an delightfully light and nourishing supper as well as an gracious side dish, especially when you want something different from the normal. And by the way, it is a good way to use left-over potatoes.

Luana

- 2 cans Tuna with Oil
- 4 smallish Potatoes (or 2 large)
- 2 Tbs Mayonnaise
- 2 Tbs Juice from Pickles
- 2-4 Sundried Tomatoes
- 2 Artichokes, canned
- 1-2 Carrots, boiled
  - Dill
  - Italian Parsley
  - Chives
- 1 Tbs Capers
- 1 Medium Pickles, chopped

Boil the potatoes and carrots. Slice them or cube them, however you like.

When you open your tuna cans, you can pour most of the oil away, but leave some of it to give a fuller taste to the salad. Mix the tuna with the potatoes and carrots. Add the mayonnaise. If you prefer not to use the mayonnaise you can use all the oil from the tuna cans and add more juice from the pickles.

Mix in the parsley, capers, pickle, sundried tomatoes, chopped chives and artichokes.

In Italy it is hard to find anything but superb cooking. The only exceptions might be found around some of the tourist attractions in Rome. Even in those restaurants, however, the cooks are not bad - just sometimes indifferent to the tourists. Go to a restaurant where only Italians frequent, and the standards are the highest. Take for example the Rome airport. For many years, the food vendors around the international gates offered so-so things to eat. But at the domestic gates, where Italian passengers ate, the food was best quality.

Cuisine is important to every Italian and there is little patience for halfhearted attempts in the kitchen. But often, even the best Italian dishes are done in simplicity, just like this salad from Luana. You can see her other recipes elsewhere in *The Nomad Chef*.

In Italy everything is realized in a way that plays to your senses, whether it's the simple Caprese Salad Michael ordered in a small Venetian trattoria, the ceiling of our Trastevere home in Rome, or an evening piano concert amidst the columns of Rome's ancient Teatro di Marcello.

My favorite Greek market in Kolonaki, downtown Athens

Vegetables and Rice

Croquette Potatoes
from Peter's kitchen, Greece

Servings: 20 croquettes

Try these flavorful croquettes, one of chef Peter's specialties. They go well alongside many of the other recipes in The Nomad Chef.

Peter

- 1 ½ lbs Potatoes
- ¼ cup Parmesan Cheese
- 2 Eggs
- Breadcrumbs
- Flour
- 1 Tb Milk
- 1 tsp Nutmeg
- 1 tsp Salt
- Pepper
- Oil for frying (Sunflower Oil, if possible)

Peel the potatoes, cut them into quarters, and cook them covered in salted water for 15 to 20 minutes, or until soft. Now, drain the potatoes and return them to the hotplate to dry by shaking the pan back and forth over the heat for a moment or two. Make sure that the steam goes away. No wetness is allowed at all.

Mash the potatoes in the pan. Add salt, a dash of nutmeg, 1 egg yolk. (save the egg white), and the Parmesan cheese. Cool the mixture and shape into small 1-inch long rolls, coating them in flour. Dip the croquettes into a mixture of the beaten egg plus the remaining egg white and milk. Then coat them with fine breadcrumbs.

Deep fry in hot oil (370 F) until golden brown. Drain on absorbent paper. If you wish, add some crushed garlic and chopped chives to the mixture.

    During the first of our two tours in Athens, Peter catered a sit-down dinner or reception once a month in our home. I learned a lot from him about how to manage large events. Peter called me a week ahead to give me the ingredients list. He wanted everything on the kitchen counter when he arrived the morning of the party.
    Scrambling through Athens' chaotic traffic to the supermarket was sometimes a big challenge. Occasionally, the entire city center was closed due to heavy pollution. Once I got caught for hours in a huge jam when I drove into a neighborhood where terrorists had just assassinated a top political leader. Terrorists, pollution, and wild drivers notwithstanding, Peter's events were works of perfection. More about Peter elsewhere in *The Nomad Chef*.

Egyptian Rice

Servings: makes 2 cups

from Paulette's kitchen, Egypt

Often your technique makes the dish. Take this remarkable Egyptian Rice, for example. All it has is rice, water, and butter, but look at the difference when you follow our Egyptian friend Paulette's recipe. Also note the two variations, one for rice vermicellini, and the other for chicken rice. They are all very simple and delicious if you follow the technique. The recipe makes enough for two adults. Multiply it accordingly to make a sufficient amount for the number of guests. (For another simple but remarkable recipe, see Paulette's French Baby Peas recipes next in The Nomad Chef.)

Paulette

½ cup White Rice (Barilla or similar rice)

2 Tbs Butter (or Olive Oil)

1 Tb Salt

Vermicelli or Vermicellini (or Angel's Hair Pasta) for Rice Vermicellini

Chicken broth for Chicken Rice

Rice
Place the quantity of rice you want in a bowl and wash it in cold tap water until the water runs clear – about 3 rinses should be enough. Then pour enough boiling water into the bowl to cover the washed rice, and add salt. Let sit for at least 30 minutes.

Melt the butter. When melted (don't let it get brown), pour in a quantity of water equal to the amount of rice you are preparing plus a quarter cup more, and bring to a boil.

Drain the rice, which has been standing in salted water, and pour it into the melted butter and water. Put the lid on the saucepan and let boil for approximately 7 minutes. You can lift the lid occasionally to see how the cooking is progressing. When the rice has absorbed all the liquid in the pan, the surface will be covered with little depressions. Put the lid on again, turn the heat to as low as possible, and let cook for 15 minutes. (During that time don't lift the lid, as it will release the steam that will cook the rice). If you have a timer, set it for 15 minutes to remind you.

Variation 1: Rice Vermicellini
When you have melted the margarine in the saucepan, add vermicellini (about ¼ the quantity of the rice you are preparing) and brown them until they are fairly dark, but be careful not to burn. (You will probably need more than 2 tablespoons butter, depending, of course, on the amount of rice you are cooking. The basic rule is that you need enough butter to brown the vermicellini.) The vermicellini must be broken between your fingers into small pieces before cooking. Then add the water as before and follow the same procedures as in the Rice section above. However, you will need to add a bit more water.

Variation 2: Chicken Rice
Use broth left from cooking a chicken, or ready broth, instead of the plain water, to boil the rice. Chicken rice has an excellent flavor.

Note: It doesn't matter if you leave the rice to soak longer than 30 minutes, but it should not be soaked less. During the soaking, prepare the rest of the meal, or relax for a few moments.

For centuries the Mediterranean has been a popular destination for wanderers from Europe and elsewhere. The warm summer evenings by the sea and mild winters, of course, attract everyone. But dishes like this one are found in all the surrounding countries. There are so many unforgettable meals, often done with simplicity, on tables everywhere from Gibraltar to Greece to Egypt. When it gets down to it, it's the food and the people who enjoy it with you that make the evenings.

French Baby Peas

from Paulette's kitchen, Egypt

Servings: 4

This is another recipe from Paullette. Her peas are just as heaven should be: simple to make and divine to eat.

Paulette

- 2 cups Peas, fresh or frozen
- 1 Onion
- Lettuce leaves
- 1-2 Tbs Butter

Use fresh peas, if possible, but frozen will do. Line a saucepan on the bottom and sides with lettuce leaves. Peel and slice the onion. Place the peas between the lettuce and onions. Salt and pepper to taste.

Add 1 tablespoon of butter on top. Cover the saucepan. Cook slowly over a medium heat, but avoid lifting the lid while cooking, since the peas are cooked by steam – the moisture is provided by the lettuce leaves and the peas themselves. Remove as soon as they are soft. I often add an additional tablespoon of butter after the peas have been cooked.

It takes approximately 10-15 minutes to cook frozen peas. I mix everything together and serve it on a platter or dish. You can also separate the onions and lettuce to serve the peas alone.

    I remember with much fondness the wonderful afternoon when Paulette had us to lunch in Milan, Italy. Her apartment windows were open to allow in a breeze. The lush trees lining the streets ushered visual freshness into the room. Everything was so gracefully done, like these peas.
    It was her gift to us, that afternoon, and with this recipe we have something from Paulette that will never disappear.   (You will read more about Paulette in the recipe for "Supreme au Chocolat.")

Italian Baked Tomatoes

Servings: 4

from Simone's kitchen, Italy

Italians like light food, and Simone, our Roman chef, used to fix these baked tomatoes for me often. This is a classy vegetable dish to serve alongside your favorite main course. Couldn't be easier!

Simone

- 2 Large Tomatoes
- 4 Basil Leaves, crumbled, or 4 tsp dried Basil
- Salt
- Pepper
- 4 tsp Extra Virgin Olive Oil
- 4 Tbs Breadcrumbs (Panko, seasoned Italian, or ordinary breadcrumbs)

Halve the tomatoes and drizzle half the olive oil over them. Salt and Pepper. Mix together the crumbs, basil, the remainder of the oil, and some additional salt and pepper.

If you use Italian bread crumbs, don't mix the salt and pepper with the crumbs. Rather, only slightly salt and pepper the tomato before putting the Italian breadcrumbs on top.

Arrange the mixture on the top of the cut tomato halves and bake on a lightly oiled dish in a preheated 400 F oven for 40 minutes. The crumbs should have a nice brown color.

My "Tomato Stall Man" from the Testaccio Market in Rome

What would Italian dishes be without tomatoes! Think of the pastas, lasagnas, vegetable dishes, and salads, made with tomatoes, that we call *Italian Food*. Traditionally that is not how it was. Tomatoes are from the Americas and did not arrive in Europe until the Italian Renaissance was well under way. Medieval Italian food must have been more white than red.

Today, tomatoes are an art in Italy. (For that matter just about anything having to do with food in Italy is an art.) In Rome, for example, there was a century old market called Testaccio which had indoor and outdoor shops daily selling food and many other articles. As you wandered through the Testaccio Market you got a fantastic glimpse of everyday Roman life, such as a stall which specialized only in tomatoes. There were maybe 45 varieties of tomatoes. You told the owner, with his long pony tail, what you were making, and he advised you which tomato was best for your dish. This was serious. He once refused to sell me tomatoes that he said were the wrong ones for the dish that I was making!

The next recipe is for stuffed tomatoes done with a Greek method that is also very tasty, but slightly heavier. And see more about Simone, the author of my Italian Baked Tomatoes recipe, and some of his other recipes in *The Nomad Chef*.

Mykonian Stuffed Tomatoes

Servings: 6

from Violetta's kitchen, Greece

Not many people go to Mykonos to get recipes. That is not why I went, but that is what I did. I learned how to make these delightful Greek stuffed tomatoes and stuffed peppers in Mykonos. You can serve them as an opening first course or as a side to a main course. Nowadays, when many people are careful about their diet and try to eat less meat, this dish can be a simple main course as well. Don't hesitate to cook them one day, refrigerate, and warm them up for the next day's meal. Use the same filling to make stuffed green peppers, or for variety you can make half tomatoes and half peppers.

Violetta and her husband Nikos

6 Large Tomatoes

1/2 cup Uncooked Rice (Carolina or Arborio Rice)

½ Onion

Fresh Parsley (if available)

Fresh Mint (if available)

1/2 cup Olive Oil

3/4 tsp Salt

1/2 tsp Black Pepper

1/2 cup Black Grapes (small)

Optional: half a handful of Breadcrumbs

Carefully slice off the tops of the tomatoes (about a fourth way from the tops of the tomatoes) and set them aside. Remove the inside of the tomatoes carefully without breaking the shells and chop the filling into small pieces. Drain the tomatoes upside down for 15 min. Add to this mixture your chopped onion, parsley, mint, salt, pepper, rice and ¾ cup olive oil. Mix well. Mykoneans sometimes also add chopped grapes to the mixture. You can let the mixture stand for ½ hour before filling.

Now sprinkle some salt inside each tomato and fill the tomatoes with the mixture. Place the filled tomatoes on a cooking pan and put the cut tomato tops on top the stuffed tomatoes, or, alternatively, sprinkle them with breadcrumbs. If you wish, spread some olive oil with your finger on the outside of the tomatoes. Pour the leftover olive oil on top of the tomatoes. You may use some additional oil according to taste. If your tomatoes are not very juicy you might have to add some water to bottom of the pan. Bake in a preheated 350 F oven about 1 hour or until the rice is done. Let the tomatoes sit in the warm oven for a while after the temperature has been turned off, or if you need your oven for other purposes let them sit for 15 minutes on the countertop to soften the skin.

P.S. An excellent variation on this recipe is to cook the filling as a side dish to a meat course, chopping a few tomatoes inside it.

Violetta was from Mykonos. With its old white cubic Cycladic houses and shops and magnificent beaches, Mykonos is in my view the princess of all Greek islands. It is also a chic meeting point for the international jet set. Before going there the first time, I thought it might be superficial – and many Greeks think it is – but for me it was love at first sight, and we went back to visit many times.

On one of those visits I got this recipe from Violetta. We met her at her family's restaurant on one of Mykonos's lovely secluded beaches. We were staying in a small but cozy hotel next door. It was about half an hour drive from Mykonos town, so we had to take a boat taxi or bus to get there. There were two brothers and their families. One ran the hotel. And Violetta and her husband had a charming taverna that was surrounded by lovely green gardens and colorful flowers. Next to it, "Papous," the grandfather, sat comfortably in the shade of the vine-covered veranda, watching and giving advice. Violetta worked in the kitchen, and her husband Nikos was at the cash register.

When she was younger, Violetta studied economics in Athens. After getting her degree, however, she faced a dilemma: "Either Nikos or the books," as she put it. A romantic at heart, Violetta chose Nikos. Violetta had been working for the family business 20 years when I asked her how she felt about her decision. She laughed and said: "I don't like it, but what can I do? It is a custom and always done this way." So we had Violetta's stuffed tomatoes and peppers, in the veranda shade, a breeze blowing across the beach. And Nikos got Violetta, quite a treasure, and lucky for us and anyone who visits their taverna.

Red Lentil Curry *("Dahl")*
from Kamala's kitchen, Sri Lanka

Servings: 6-8

If you like Indian food, you will love this aromatic Sri Lankan vegetable curry called "Dahl." It makes a delicious and memorable side to many main courses.

Kamala

- 3/4 cup Red Lentils
- 1 sprig Curry leaf (optional)
- 3 Garlic Cloves
- 1 inch Ginger Root
- ¼ Onion
- 1 tsp Turmeric
- ¼ tsp Chili Powder
- 1-2 Tbs Olive Oil
- 1 tsp Curry Powder
- 2 inches Cinnamon Stick
- 5 oz Spinach
- Salt
- ¾ cup Coconut Milk, warm

First, wash the lentils. Then, chop the garlic and onions and cut the ginger into thin slices. Fry all three in the olive oil. Now, add the lentils to a pan with the onions and ginger. Throw in the curry leaves and the spices. Add enough water to cover all the ingredients. Put on a medium heat and start to cook the "Dahl." Keep stirring frequently, and after a short while add the coconut milk.

It takes about 30 minutes to break down the lentils to have a soup consistency. Keep an eye on the liquid. If the lentils are not done yet but the liquid has begun to disappear, you might want to add more water. Toward the end of the cooking add the spinach. Stir well and continue to cook for 2-3 minutes. Salt to taste.

    This is another of the excellent recipes received from my good Sri Lankan friend, Kamala. Enjoy it along with her other Sri Lankan Rice and Eggplant Salad recipes in *The Nomad Chef*).

    One afternoon I got together with Kamala to see firsthand how to prepare this and other Sri Lankan dishes. In the middle of our preparations, her anesthesiologist husband Neville, arrived home from the hospital. He announced "I saved four lives today but you saved leftovers." Neville is known for his keen humor. While Neville kept us entertained we finished everything for the meal in two hours.

    I came home to change my clothes and pick up Michael. We returned an hour later to enjoy a most wonderful evening and good meal together with Kamala and Neville.

Savory Potatoes

from Simone's kitchen, Italy

Servings: 2

My Italian chef Simone often served these fried potatoes with an Italian flair. They go well alongside any meat dish. As much as we loved pasta, the potatoes were always a welcome change.

Simone

- 2 Large Potatoes
- Extra virgin Olive Oil
- 1 Garlic Clove cut in pieces
- Fresh or dried Rosemary
- Salt, Pepper

Peel and cut the potatoes into 1/2 inch slices. Cut the garlic clove into pieces. Pour some oil into a large frying pan (or electric skillet) and sauté the garlic for a short while. Then add the potatoes, salt and pepper, and cover the pan, cooking over a medium heat.

Cook without lifting the lid until a crust forms on the outside of the potatoes, about 10-15 minutes. Turn them over and add the rosemary that you have crushed in a mortar or food processor, to taste. Cook another 10-15 minutes so that a crust forms on both sides.

Remove the garlic pieces, and you are ready!

    Potatoes do well in Finnish soil, and I grew up eating potato dishes. There is a long winter in Finland, but the short summer growing season of the far north is long enough for them to ripen before the winter frosts. Today, Nordic shops are full of good fresh vegetables and fruits, but before fast inexpensive transportation made that possible, potatoes were a mainstay in the North.

    When they first came to Finland from South America, potatoes had to sell themselves. Many in the churches found them unacceptable, even sinful, growing as they did underground, much closer to the devil's underworld, some said. Potatoes finally gained popularity in Finland during the 1700's when pastors praised potatoes over the pulpit in order to combat the all too common hunger and malnutrition found among their congregations.

    My husband Mike, who is from Idaho, used to tell me that potatoes where he grew up were so big that sometimes it took a truck to carry one potato. I didn't know whether I believed him, but when I visited there the first time, he bought me a postcard depicting a large truck with a single potato on its long bed.

    Joking aside, residents of Idaho can be proud of their large, tasty potatoes that are famous due to the volcanic soil they grow in. People in Idaho bragged to me that President Reagan used to fly Idaho "spuds" to White House dinners, but I suspect his cook bought them from the local Washington supermarkets like I have. Whether you grow your own potatoes, buy them at the supermarket, or ship them in from Idaho, try this potato dish, another I received from Simone.

Sri Lankan Rice

from Kamala's kitchen, Sri Lanka

Servings: 12-16

This recipe is more than simply another way to do steamed rice. Serve it as a side dish full of exotic flavors and aromas.

- 3 cups Rice, Basmati or Jasmine
- 2 Tbs Butter
- 2 Tbs Olive Oil
- 2 Onions
- 3 Garlic Cloves, crushed
- 2 tsp Saffron
- 1 Sprig Curry leaves (if available)
- 1 tsp Salt
- Pepper
- 1 Stick Cinnamon
- ½ tsp Cardamom
- 2 Cloves, whole
- A handful Cashews, sautéed
- A handful Raisins
- ¾ cup Peas, frozen
- 1 cup Coconut milk

Kamala

First, wash the rice well until the water running through it is clear. This requires about 4-5 rinses. Drain and set aside.

Next, chop and saute one quarter of your onion and the garlic in the olive oil and butter. Add the saffron and curry leaves. Stir and cook a minute or two, and then add your rice. Stirring again, fry the rice until it gets some color. Remove the rice mixture to your rice cooker and add the water, salt, pepper, cinnamon stick, cloves, and cardamom. While the rice is cooking put your frozen peas into cold water in a separate pan. As soon as they are thawed, drain the water off and set aside.

Sauté the cashews and raisins in a frying pan with olive oil. Remove. Fry the rest of the onions cut into slices. The color should be quite dark but not burned. When the rice is ready, place it on a serving dish, fold in the peas, and decorate with the onions, raisins, and cashews.

Wonderful recipes such as this one from Kamala bring into your home exotic tastes and aromas that only the rich could afford in centuries past.

Some say that people have been using spices since 50,000 BC. I know that spices were being traded 2,000 BC throughout Asia and Mediterranean. I once visited Acrotiri, a town on the Greek island of Santorini, where a volcanic eruption nearly 4000 years ago quickly covered everything, including the giant amphoras that stored their food. When the town was unearthed some years ago, remnants of the same foods grown on the island today lay in the bottom of these ancient vases. A fresco on the wall of one of the remaining homes depicted saffron gatherers.

So some of the most important building blocks in our cuisine may be as old as civilization. Spicy aromatic dishes such as this one always seem to join me to this long and distinguished food tradition

Remnants at the bottom of Amphoras in Santorini's ancient Acrotiri tell us how long many of our food traditions can be

I love visiting markets. My earliest memories of markets go back to my childhood when we regularly shopped the booths of the market square in my home town in Finland. As I wandered the busy passages between the rows of booths, I heard accordion music playing and people singing, attracting people to the square. We would often bring home a *Viipurin Rinkeli*, a pretzel shaped bread. My parents, grandparents, and I then gathered around the table, pulling off pieces of the freshly baked loaf and sharing news we heard in town. The market was not just a place to buy fresh vegetables, berries, and pastries, but where we got latest gossip from the friends and relatives we met there.

Breads and Pastries

Beebop-a-Reebop Rhubarb Pie

Servings: 12

from the "Savo" kitchen, Finland

This is a scrumptious recipe to make with rhubarb from the summer garden or supermarket. It is called a pie, but is more in the fashion of a sponge cake, wonderfully refreshing for a dessert or on the coffee table any time of the year. Try it and you will love it.

3 Eggs

1 ¼ cups Sugar

5 oz Butter

¾ cup Milk

1 2/3 cups Flour

3 tsp Baking Powder

4 cups Rhubarb, chopped fresh or frozen

Some additional Sugar

optional: strawberries, chopped almonds

Whip the eggs and sugar together. Heat the butter and milk in a sauce pan on the stove, but don't boil. After the milk and butter have cooled down a bit, you can mix it together with your egg-sugar mixture. Mix flour and baking powder together and combine with the above mixture

Pour everything onto an oil-sprayed 8 x 12 in. Pyrex dish or two round Pyrex dishes, and evenly spread the rhubarb over the top. For a tasty variation, add strawberries to your rhubarb.

Bake in a preheated oven at 375 F for about 15 minutes. Now sprinkle some sugar over the pie. If you wish you can also top the pie with chopped almonds after sprinkling the sugar. Continue to bake still another 15 minutes or until it is done.

I was totally delighted the first time I heard Garrison Keillor jokingly sing his Beebop-a-Reebop Rhubarb Pie song in "A Prairie Home Companion." When it ended "...*Mama's little baby loves rhubarb, rhubarb, rhubarb pie,"* I thought, *This Mama's Baby* does love rhubarb pie. It's actually delicious, and I think you will like it, too, if you haven't tried it. The fun-filled lyrics, written by Garrison Keillor, reveal his Scandinavian background. Rhubarb grows quickly in the gardens of Scandinavia, and in Garrison's Minnesota, as well. Sour as a lemon when eaten raw, it makes delicious cooked dishes - especially sweet ones!

I got this recipe from friends who lived in a region in central Finland called Savo. That is probably the reason why when I make it I am always reminded of my Finnish grandmother, Selma, who was from Savo. Selma wasn't talkative like most people from Savo are, but she was hard working and a good cook. She had long white hair braided in a bun, and when she let it down I saw it reached all the way to her thighs. As a small girl I wondered how long it might have taken to grow so long. Every night before I went to bed, Selma had a plate full of delicacies waiting for me. This was fine during my early childhood, but as I grew older I became weight conscious and tried to save her "love on a plate" for morning. I didn't always manage.

My father was a wonderful rhubarb grower. His strong tall stalks grew at the back of the garden. He carried left over water from cooked vegetables as well as the peelings from fruit and vegetables to fertilize his rhubarb plants. He said that this was what made it grow so well. And strong rhubarb stalks made good rhubarb pie.

Selma, me in her arms, stands before our badly damaged home in Viipuri following a bombing by Russian planes in WWII.

Chocolate Brownies

from Ian's kitchen, Italy

Servings: 8

No one has ever eaten better brownies than these. Ian developed the recipe himself.

Ian

- 1 ¾ cups Sugar
- 3 Eggs
- ¾ cup Butter, melted
- ¾ cup Swiss Cocoa Powder
- ¾ cup Flour
- 7 oz Swiss Dark Chocolate
- ¾ cup Hazel Nuts (or other nuts), chopped finely
- 4 oz White Chocolate

Start by beating the eggs, add the sugar, and then continue beating. Now, stir in the melted butter that has cooled. Mix the flour and cocoa powder together. Melt the dark chocolate in a double boiler. Add the chocolate and the well-chopped nuts to the flour mixture. (If the nuts are not chopped well, the brownies crumble when you cut them into squares.) Combine the two mixtures. Break the white chocolate into little pieces and fold in.

Butter well an 8 x 8 in. baking pan. Spread the dough evenly in the pan and bake it at 375 F for 35 minutes. The texture will look undone when you stick your toothpick in -- this recipe is full of chocolate, that's why. When the brownies cool, it will harden.

If you want moist brownies bake them 30 minutes; a drier texture, bake for 40 minutes.

Slice the brownies carefully with a small sharp knife and lift them out with a spatula to avoid breakage. They taste delicious, but break easily.

There are three American embassies in Rome: to the Republic of Italy, to the Vatican, and to the United Nations. Ian worked for the American ambassador to the UN, and often, when the ambassador was away, he worked in my kitchen alongside my regular chef, Simone. I consider myself fortunate to share a kitchen with Ian and to have become friends. He was a Scottish gentleman and world class chef.

I first tasted these brownies at a buffet. There were diplomats from all over the world, many of them in their colorful native dress, all joining to eat Ian's brownies! When I took my first bite, I knew I needed the recipe for my cookbook. Ian said he wouldn't give it to anybody in Italy because he sells these brownies during special seasons. But after I coaxed and begged long enough (about six months of reminding him), Ian generously gave me the right to share the recipe. Here you go.

Chocolate Chip Cookies

from Lorilee's kitchen, Utah

Servings: 3 dozen

Chocolate chip cookies must be one of the most baked things in America. I never mastered making them until I got this exceptional recipe from my sister-in-law Lorilee. They rise in the oven and when you take them out they will keep their puffy texture and won't collapse like so many chocolate chip cookies do.

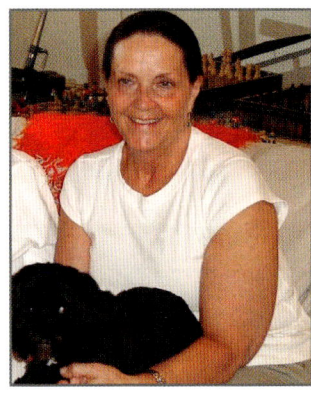

Lorilee

- 1 ½ cups Sugar
- 1 ½ cups Brown Sugar
- 1 lb Butter
- 4 Eggs
- 2 tsp Salt
- 2 tsp Soda
- 2 tsp Vanilla Extract
- 6 ¾ cups Flour (heaping)
- 1 ½ - 2 12-oz packages Chocolate Chips

Mix all the ingredients together very well. (I take my butter out hours before baking so it will soften nicely in the room temperature). Add the flour. Mix well.

Now, add the chocolate chips. Use a tablespoon to drop them onto a cookie sheet, about 2 inches apart. Bake 10 minutes at 375 F or until just brown. The key is to take your cookies out when they are starting to brown but still seem a little bit undone. That way they will remain moist.

Note: I often add only part of the flour with a kitchen machine and the rest, by hand. They turn out nicer that way.

    Fine cooking doesn't age. Good recipes have been passed down for generations. But not just old recipes stay alive. New ones are born and can enter the family tradition and give joy to new generations.

    Take this wonderful recipe, for example. Many years ago, Mike's sister Lorilee developed a recipe for full-bodied, rich chocolate cookies that are exceptional in texture and taste. She shared them with us. Now her children, our children, and other cousins serve these cookies in their homes. My son-in-law even knows the recipe by heart.

    Lorilee began a family tradition, an important accomplishment in this day when such traditions are easily forgotten! This wasn't especially easy in Lorilee's case, for she had to raise a large family virtually on her own while she studied to finish college. Today, she is vice president of a large bank. And she still makes these nicely textured cookies (and many other tasty dishes) for family occasions.

Chocolate Roll Cookies
from Salme's kitchen, Finland

Servings: about 15-18 cookies

This is not an overly sweet cookie, but it is easy and fast to make, requiring maybe only 15-20 minutes' preparation time.

Salme and her grand daughters

- 1 ¼ cup Flour
- 2/3 cup Sugar
- 1 Tb Cocoa
- ½ tsp Vanilla (sugar)
- ½ tsp Baking Powder
- ¼ cup Butter
- 2 small Eggs (one for the mixture, the other for brushing)
- 1/4 Almonds, slivered or chopped

Mix flour, vanilla, cocoa, and baking powder into one bowl. In another, cream butter, sugar, and 1 of your eggs. (You can add some extra sugar for a sweeter taste.) Mix the two together thoroughly, and then divide the dough into 3 portions and roll them into thick rolls. Before rolling, dust the working surface with flour.

Place on a cookie sheet covered with parchment baking paper. Brush with 1 whipped egg and sprinkle with slivered almonds or pearl sugar (crumbled sugar cubes).

Bake at 375 F for about 10 minutes until done. While still warm, cut diagonally into small squares.

My Finnish godmother Salme probably made better pastries than anyone I know. She was only 13 when she was orphaned, but she went to a home economics school and became a marvelous baker. At the end of World War II, Salme, like my family, was forced to abandon her home forever. She and her husband, Tauno, had always been close friends with my parents, and came as refugees to Lahti, Finland, where we also had evacuated. She was like another grandmother to me.

It was not too long a walk from my house to Salme's, and we often took a path through the woods to get there. Especially in the wintertime it was an adventure because we were all bundled up against the cold. We took off our snowy boots, hats, gloves, and coats by the stove in Salme's warm kitchen where they would dry. Meanwhile, Salme would pull from the cupboard many different goodies which we enjoyed with warm blackcurrant juice. Life must have been so much more relaxed then, for it was common to have something always prepared for surprise visitors. There was even a word in Finnish for it, *vierasvara*, which meant something for visitors. Years later, my childhood tradition continued as I walked with my children through the snowy wintry evenings from my parents place to Salme's, eager to enjoy her *vierasvara*.

Christmas Tarts
from my own kitchen

Servings: 18 tarts

Once you have tried these Finnish Christmas Tarts ("Joulutorttuja"), you will not want Christmas without them. They are in the form of stars and smell divine when they come out of the oven. After you decorate the tarts with powdered sugar, they are as pretty and delicate as a Christmas star should be. My mother might not have approved of my modern version for the pastry. She always made her own dough, but when time is limited we can take short cuts. And this one really works. These tarts are so easy you can make them with your children or grandchildren. In fact, I once made Christmas Stars together with our five-year old grandson. It was a joy to see him put the plum filling on the center of the tarts and to see his hand reach out to take the first bite when it was still warm in his hand.

- 1 package Puff Pastry (frozen sheets)
- Powdered Sugar
- 1 lb Pitted Prunes
- 3 cups Water
- ¾ cup Sugar or less if you wish
- 2-3 Tbs Lemon Juice

Filling
Cover the prunes with water and cook in a sauce pan about 15 to 20 minutes. You need to stir regularly until the prunes have separated into a smallish mass. Now puree in your processor into a fine texture. Season with the sugar and lemon juice.

Pastry
Take the puff pastry at room temperature. The package has 2 separate rolls of pastry. Open the first and divide it by cutting with a sharp knife into 3 long and equal strips. Cut each one of these strips into 3 equal square pieces to make altogether 9 squares. Cut a slit into each square from each of its 4 corners toward the center leaving in the middle an uncut space that you fill with a full teaspoon of the prune filling. Fold every other corner towards the center with the tips resting on top each other on top of the filling. Press the tips down well. This way you make your square into a star.

Now carefully lift these stars onto a cookie sheet covered with parchment paper. I brush the tarts with a beaten egg to give them a nice color. Bake in a hot preheated oven at 400 F for about 10-15 minutes until they are golden. After removing them, sprinkle some powdered sugar through a small hand sieve or flour sifter.

Five-year old Jesse was an excellent Christmas Tarts chef

My mother's name was "Lempi Tuulikki" which in Finnish means "A Breeze of Love." In the tradition of her name, she breezed about the small kitchen that she shared with my grandmother Selma. Her holiday kitchen was always filled with the aroma of freshly baked Christmas tarts. She began baking them in the beginning of December at the start of the country's long Christmas celebration. She was always ready for the many Christmas parties in schools, offices, neighborhoods, and wherever friends could get together.

Early in our family life I wanted to follow Lempi's example, but I found the Holiday season so busy that it seemed I was always behind schedule. To avoid the stress I put together a Christmas Tart recipe that was quick and easy. I wanted tasty Christmas pastries ready in "a wink of the eye and a twist of the head." I found it was convenient to have the ingredients pre-made and ready to bake at virtually a moment's notice.

Normally, I double or triple the filling recipe, make it ahead of time, and place it in the refrigerator. I also keep a supply of puff pastry in my freezer. When I have a free morning I prepare tarts to take to friends on the same day. I often end up making around 300 tarts each Christmas. This might seem a lot, but the preparation and baking are done separately over a longer period, and the amount of time needed for a single day's batch is not much.

You can also store the tarts in a carefully packed container, ready to use anytime. I lay wax paper between the layers to prevent them from sticking to each other. Of course when you serve them you might want to warm the tarts just a little in a microwave or in the oven, and then redecorate them with powdered sugar.

Coconut Cookies
from Salme's kitchen, Finland

Servings: about 16 cookies

This is the second of two delicious cookie recipes from my godmother, Salme, that I am including in this book. They both are wonderfully simple and unforgettable.

Salme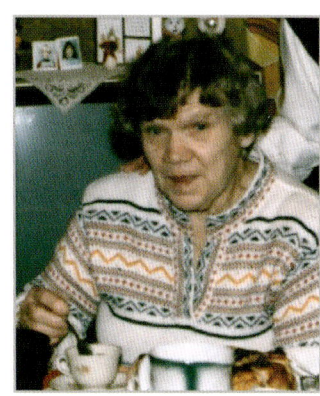

1¾ cups Butter

1 1/3 cups Sugar

6 oz Coconut, shredded

4 cups All Purpose Flour

2 tsp Baking Powder

Cream the butter and sugar well. Sift in the baking powder and flour. Add the coconut. Spoon small pieces of dough onto a cookie sheet covered with parchment paper. Make them small.

Bake at 350 F. for 15-20 minutes until light brown.

     I grew up with Karelian traditions that greatly influenced my attitudes, especially toward good food and entertaining. The Karelians are a tribe from the eastern province of Finland. They are generally gregarious and known for their gracious hospitality. Karelians love to cook and bake, and when you have food you want to share it... and have a party! Having guests to dinner, no matter how little we had, was commonplace in my home. Just look at this photo of a party at my home - how did we fit into the house? And it was winter outside.

Cowboy Cookies
from Karelia's kitchen, Virginia

Servings: About 5 dozen

From 14- year old Karelia, this is a delicious kids' recipe that has a little bit of everything nice. It also produces a large batch of cookies that you can eat, share, and freeze for a busy day.

Karelia

1 ¼ tsp Vanilla Extract

¾ cup Shortening

½ cup Butter

1 cup Sugar

1 cup Brown Sugar

3 Eggs

2 cups Flour

2 cups Oatmeal

1 1/8 tsp Baking Soda

¾ tsp Salt

6 oz. Chocolate Chips

3 oz. White Chocolate Chips

½ Cup Coconut, shredded

Mix your butter, shortening, eggs, sugars, and vanilla in a mixer. Combine the dry ingredients in a large bowl, and then mix the wet ingredients with your dry. Spoon the cookie dough onto a sheet. They will expand a lot during baking, so don't make them too large.

Bake at 350 F for 10-12 minutes

One afternoon when we stopped by our daughter Kristiina's home in northern Virginia we were greeted with the smell of cowboy cookies still in the oven. Our 14-year old granddaughter, Karelia, pulled out the cookie sheet. She had made them!

Karelia is our first grandchild. Her unique name comes from Finland's Karelia region, in Finnish tradition a home of song and music. Karelia is true to her name. The playful joyous sounds of her flute, and the deep strains of the cello she also plays contrast with each other, just like the red and black of Finnish Karelia's coat of arms.

I was fascinated to hear the background of her cookie recipe. Karelia had an exceptional English teacher in the 6th grade. This teacher inspired her to love English by showing how classic children's books and stories could teach much about the fundamentals of reading and writing. The next year when Karelia was working on a community service project together with the same wonderful teacher, they exchanged treats. She gave her teacher red velvet cupcakes that her mother had made and received two of these cookies in return. "From the moment that cookie entered my mouth, I knew that I needed the recipe," Karelia said, clearly taking after her grandmother! So they agreed to exchange recipes. "Whenever I eat this cookie, I feel grateful for teachers who try hard to make school inspiring and fun," Karelia told me.

I kissed this young baker. She deserved it!

Finnish Cinnamon Rolls & Pulla

from my own kitchen

Servings: 20-24 rolls, or 3 good sized loaves

These cinnamon rolls are called "Korvapuusti" in Finnish, which literally translated means "slaps on the ear," in reference to their shape when baked! They are beautiful, functional, and exceptionally good. With the same recipe you can make braided loaves of Finnish sweet bread, called "Pulla." No one ever forgets this queen of all sweet breads, nor these delicious rolls. The cardamom gives them their distinct festive flavor.

While the recipe makes up to 24 cinnamon rolls or 3 loaves of pulla, a lot you might think, you will find that everything disappears faster than you expect. These rolls and loaves also freeze very well. It is fun to take them from the freezer, one by one, according to your craving. Or when unexpected friends stop by, you always have something nice to offer.

Dough
- 2 cups Milk
- 2 packages, ¼ oz each, Yeast
- 2 tsp Salt
- 3 tsp Cardamom
- 1 cup Sugar
- 2 Eggs plus 1 Egg Yolk
- 6-7 ½ cups Flour
- 1 cube Butter, softened
- ½ cup Canola Oil

Filling
- 1 - 2 cubes Butter, depending on your personal taste
- ½ - 1 cup Sugar
- 3-4 tsp Cinnamon.

Dough
Add your yeast to ¾ cup of the lukewarm milk (it must be lukewarm) and one teaspoon of sugar to activate it more quickly.

Place the butter, oil, sugar, cardamom, and salt in a large mixing bowl. Heat the rest of the milk almost to a boil, and then pour it over the ingredients in your mixing bowl. Stir and then let cool. Add the eggs, and beat. Now add in the yeast mixture and start adding some of the flour little by little.

You can do this in a kitchen machine, with a hand electric mixer, or by hand with a large spoon. Keep adding more flour and if you are using a kitchen machine or electric hand mixer, change the mixing process when the dough starts to get difficult to handle, and finish kneading by hand. You will knead the dough until it doesn't stick to your hands any longer. Let the dough rise under the towel in a warm place in the kitchen (with no draft) about 2- 3 hours.

Finnish Sweet Bread ("Pulla")
To make this dough into loaves, first divide it into three parts. Then, divide each of these parts into three. Shape each part into a strip about 16 inches long by rolling the dough between your palms and a

Filling
1 - 2 cubes Butter, depending on your personal taste

½ - 1 cup Sugar

3-4 tsp Cinnamon.

Topping
1 Egg for brushing the rolls

Sugar Cubes crushed into tiny pieces to sprinkle on top the rolls. (You can also purchase a Scandinavian sugar called "Pearl Sugar," from Ikea's food store.)

rolling board. Braid three strips together into a straight loaf, pinch the ends together, and tuck under. Repeat for the second and third loaves.

Lift the braids onto baking sheets covered with parchment paper. Let them rise for about 20 minutes (the braids should be puffy but not doubled in size). Glaze the loaves by brushing the tops with a beaten egg and sprinkle with the pearl sugar, or sliced almonds, if you wish.

Bake at 375 F for about 30 minutes, or until the internal temperature reaches 185 F

Cinnamon Rolls

Divide your dough into two portions. Roll out 1 part into a 24 x 36 inch rectangle on a floured surface. Spread with ½ - 1 cube of softened butter. Mix the sugar and cinnamon, and then sprinkle the dough with half of the cinnamon sugar (or even more sugar if you prefer it sweeter; add cinnamon to taste.

Roll the rectangle up into a firm, long shaped roll. Cut diagonally (one slice slanted one direction, the next in the opposite, and so on) to make triangularly shaped pieces. With the pointed side up, press down across the center of the rolls with a finger so that the cut ends spread out, creating two ear-shaped sides. Place the rolls on baking sheets which have been covered with parchment paper. Brush the rolls with a beaten egg and sprinkle them with the sugar pieces. Let them rise about 30 minutes. Bake in a hot oven (400 F) for about 12-15 minutes.

There are many different pulla dough recipes, but I particularly like this one which I developed through experience. I thought I had a near perfect recipe, but in the kitchen I am always finding new things. When I was admiring the softness of the cinnamon rolls made by a long-time Finnish friend, Hanna, she gave me a hint to substitute some of the butter with canola oil. I have done that with this recipe, and both the rolls and pulla come out even nicer

My Finnish childhood was blessed with warm pulla and cinnamon rolls. As all Finns did, we had a sauna bath either on Friday evening or Saturday afternoon. After sauna we enjoyed warm and cold drinks with pulla, cinnamon rolls, or different berry pies. This was MUST for the week-end …there was no other way.

After my mother grew ill and was confined to a wheelchair, my father, Manne, prepared the pulla, and in fact became an expert pulla maker. He whipped and whipped the butter-sugar mixture until it was fluffy. He continued the same way with the flour.

Later, when my husband was finishing graduate school, I was penny-pinching mother of three babies. Out of love and desperation I started a home bakery, baking in the wee morning hours of the morning. Pulla – and the Cinnamon Rolls – were the unqualified favorite of all our customers.

Manne, inducted as hardly more than a boy, survived on the front for nearly four years, and as a prisoner of war in Russia for another, to return home to become an expert pulla baker, and most importantly, my father.

Traditionally life in Finland began and ended in a sauna house often sitting on a lake like this one. There, mothers gave birth, and loved ones were washed before burial. My father told how he came home from school one evening to hear a baby crying from the sauna. It was his new born sister. But for most Finns today the sauna bath is a weekly event that soothes the body and spirit. Afterwards, pulla or cinnamon rolls are always a welcome treat.

Graham Rolls
from Tuula's kitchen, Finland

Servings: 24-26

Everybody appreciates warm fresh rolls coming right out of the oven -- and your enjoyment is all that more when you know that what you are about to eat is healthy. These Graham Rolls fit that description perfectly.

Tuula and her husband Heikki

- 2 cups warm Water
- 4 tsp Yeast
- a pinch of Sugar
- 2 Eggs
- 2 tsp Salt
- 2 cubes Butter, soft
- ¾ cup Oats
- 2 cups Graham flour
- 2 cups or more All Purpose Flour

Mix the yeast and sugar with a small amount of water in a smallish bowl and set aside. In a mixing bowl beat together the rest of the water with eggs and salt. When you see that your yeast has activated, add it to the bowl along with the oats and graham flour. Knead the dough. Now you can add the softened butter and keep kneading more. Start to add the white flour until the texture is soft. You can test it with a dry finger and if it comes out clean, it is ready. Set your bowl in a warm place with a covered towel, and let it rise until doubled.

On a baking board divide your dough into three portions. Cut each portion into small round rolls. My rule is that if you can roll the rolls inside your palm, then it is in the right size.

Bake the rolls in the oven at 400 F for about 10-15 minutes. The baking time depends on your oven and the size of the rolls. But don't bake them too long because your rolls will be too dry. I brush the rolls with milk during the last 2 minutes of baking time. I have also turned the grill button on just for a minute or two at the end to give the rolls some color if they seem to be pale (but be careful not to let them burn). When ready they are yummy with butter and honey!

    Graham flour is a coarsely ground type of wheat flour and less processed than whole-wheat flour. It is named after Sylvester Graham, one of the pioneers of the health food movement, who invented it in 1829. You should buy it in small amounts, refrigerate the flour or keep it in an airtight containers in the freezer like I do. It has a higher oil content than whole wheat flour and may go rancid if left out too long.

    I received this nutritious recipe from my Finnish cousin, Tuula. She and her husband Heikki were hard workers and accomplished a lot. Raising four outstanding children, and both holding down full time jobs, they spent evenings building a beautiful new home with their own hands. One of the things I liked about their home was its large wood-burning stone oven in the kitchen. The oven made for a homey atmosphere, and it didn't only bake but could keep food warm for at least a day.

    This way Finns lived traditionally. In my childhood home, a masonry stove was in the main room, with my bed next to it. In the evenings after the stove was warmed, oh how I enjoyed the heat against my cold toes and the smell of the meat dishes and casseroles slowly baking to be ready the next day.

The Nomad Chef

Holiday Stollen
from Max's kitchen, Idaho

Servings: 8-12 loaves about 13 oz. each

As the Holidays arrive I am always looking for something to make for friends, family, and office. This recipe makes a batch of a festive Holiday bread called "Stollen." It does not take much longer to make many small loaves to brighten the day and the stomachs of your friends with a personal holiday greeting. That's what makes the Holidays memorable.

Sponge
1 cup warm Water

2 tsp Dry Yeast

1 tsp Malt or Sugar

2 cups Flour

Dough:
1 cup Milk

5 tsp Dry Yeast

1 ½ cups Sugar

3 tsp Salt

5 Eggs

2 ¼ cups Butter

6 cups Bread Flour

3 Tbs Cinnamon

1 Tb Cardamom

5 cups White Raisins, soaked in water

2 ½ cups Fruit (candied), soaked in rum

2 cups Nuts

(Max sometimes uses half white raisins and half dark)

Optional:
1 cup Cranberries

1 cup Dates

Max

Here is how you put everything together:

Sponge
Make the sponge mixture and let it rest about 3 hours or more. (If you can't find malt, try malted milk in the can.)

Dough
To the sponge mixture which has been standing about 3 hours, add the sugar, then flour, and then half of the butter. Mix salt together with the eggs and add to the mixture. Then add cinnamon and cardamom, and then the rest of the butter, and last, the zest from the oranges. If the dough is too soft, add more flour.

Let the dough rest about 1 ½ hours.

Filling
While the dough is resting, you can make your filling. In a food processor, combine the nuts and sugar and process until the nuts are coarsely chopped. Add the flour, butter, and egg and process just until a paste forms. Refrigerate. (The filling can be stored in an airtight container in the refrigerator for up to 3 days.)

Orange zest from 2 oranges

Filling (Frangipane):
1 cup Almonds (5 ½ oz), toasted (if you can, use slivered almonds

1/4 cup (2 oz) firmly packed Brown Sugar

2 Tbs All Purpose Flour (plain)

2 lbs Butter (unsalted), at room temperature, cut into small cubes

1 large Egg

Loaves

Form the dough into loaves (13 or 14 oz each). Next, flatten your loaves, and roll them out with the rolling pin. Place the filling in the middle of the dough. Break an egg, whip it enough to mix the texture and brush the inside of the loaves with it. This will help to hold the loaves together.

Brush the extra flour off from the loaves with a clean, dry brush. If you are tempted to make them into bigger loaves, you are taking a risk because the smaller loaves bake better. Remember that the dough is very rich, moist, and heavy. Cover your baking sheets with parchment baking paper. The loaves rise about 1/3 in size so leave enough space for them to rise. It takes about 3 hours to rise. Bake them in the oven 350 F about 20-40 minutes. You can tell their doneness by looking at the color and feeling their texture. After they come out of oven brush them with melted butter and cover with a clean cloth.

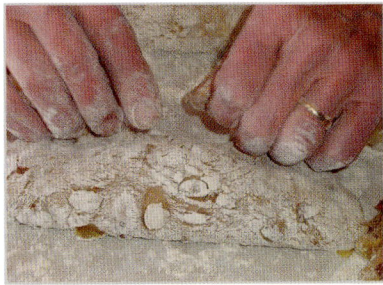 

*From my Kitchen Window
Winter Moon over
Buckskin Canyon*

When we moved to Idaho from Rome it was no surprise that we missed our favorite Italian dishes. The sweeping Rocky Mountain canyon vistas were breathtaking - but not enough. So I was delighted to meet Max who lived near us at the top of Buckskin Canyon.

Max and his Italian origin wife, Lynda, had sold their Swiss bakery in northern California and moved to Idaho three years before. He had been sweetening our mountain neighbors with his baked delicacies ever since.

Max grew up watching his father bake bread and fine pastries for their Swiss village. He told me that when he was young his German shepherd pulled a sleigh full of bread that he delivered to people in the villages. Eventually, at the age of twenty-one, he came to America where he settled in a little town in the California mountains to create chocolates, breads, and pastries.

On the day before Christmas Eve we, too, found a plate full of Max's bread and pastries on our doorstep. Among these treats was a loaf of Stollen, one of my favorite breads. Michael and I really enjoyed it - both the pastry and the neighborly idea - so I asked if Max would demonstrate how he made his Stollen, and he kindly agreed.

When we got together in his ranch house one afternoon, we saw how from his kitchen window Max could watch their horses, a donkey, several dogs, and cats prowling around the barn. I imagined this talented baker as a small boy tramping around the mountains of his hamlet in the beautiful Alps of Switzerland. And now, many years later, he was still treating the people living in our high Rocky Mountain canyon.

Idaho Potato Doughnuts
from Owen's kitchen, Idaho

Servings: about 2 ½ dozen:

My kids always thought that these are to-die-for doughnuts. I usually put them in separate individual sacks to take from the freezer when needed. Warm up in the microwave for a few seconds.

Owen

1 pkg. Dry Yeast

1 ½ cups warm Water

2/3 cup Sugar

1 tsp Salt

2/3 cup Shortening

2 Eggs

1 cup Mashed Potatoes

6 – 7 cups Flour

Glaze:
1 tsp Vanilla Extract or Lemon Juice

3 cups Powdered sugar

½ cups Water (boiling)

In a large mixing bowl dissolve the yeast in warm water. Stir in sugar, salt, shortening, eggs, potatoes (potatoes should be room temperature) and 3 cups flour. Now, beat at medium speed for 3 minutes. Mix in enough of your remaining flour by hand to make the dough easy to handle. Turn the dough out onto a well-floured surface. Knead the dough until it is smooth and elastic, about 5 minutes. Place the dough into a greased bowl and then turn it greased side up. Cover tightly and refrigerate at least 8 hours.

Next, once fully chilled, punch down your dough and on a lightly floured surface, pat it down to ¾ inch thick. Cut with floured 2 ½ inch doughnut cutter. Place the doughnuts on a lightly floured surface and let them rise for about 20-30 minutes in a warm place.

Deep-fry at 375 F (If you don't have a deep fryer you can fry them in a deep pan which has good amount of oil in it.) Deep-fry a few at a time, turning once. Fry for 2-4 minutes or until golden brown. Remove from the hot oil and drain on paper towels.

Mix your glaze ingredients until the glaze is smooth. I've also used other flavors for glazing.

While the doughnuts are warm, dip them into the glaze and place them on a cooling rack so the glaze will dry.

Good food is a time-honored greeting when we share happy moments and hardships, welcome a new family to the neighborhood, or show someone we care. It is an important tradition that creates a community around us.

I received this recipe from Mike's Idaho-born and bred Dad, Owen. Because we normally lived somewhere half way around the world, our visits to Mike's home were not as often as we liked, but when we made them we often stayed for a few weeks. I remember how always on the first morning of our visit, we woke up to the aroma of freshly baked muffins that announced a tasty breakfast waiting at the kitchen table. Mike's Dad, Owen, was at work, and it was his way of telling us he was glad we were there.

Owen grew up in Idaho's fertile Snake River Valley, home to today's delicious Idaho Russet Potato bakers. It was the Great Depression, and he was a poor farm boy. In spite of his mischievous nature, he was bright enough to graduate from his high school a year early. At 17 he joined the navy. Owen became a navy flyer and served in the Pacific after training all over the US, from Martha's Vineyard to Florida, to Hawaii. He had traveled a long way from Idaho by the time World War II ended, and it was a passage into adulthood. During his last months in uniform, he married his Idaho sweetheart, Margie, and they moved back to their hometown.

Years later, after Owen's passing, Margie told about the first time he showed her his family home that was so impoverished it had no paint. She saw him standing there, quiet, embarrassed, not knowing what to say or do. She looked up at him, took him in her arms and gave him a big kiss. It was their first kiss. And it lasted over 50 years.

Oven Pancake ("Pannukakku")

from Mari's kitchen, Finland

Servings 10 - 12

Did the milk in your fridge sour? With this recipe, you don't need to worry -- whenever you have spoiled milk you will have a good use for it. You can use fresh or sour milk in this Finnish baked pancake, "Pannukakku." Everyone loves Pannukakku topped with jams and jellies, syrup, fruit, or ice cream. You can offer it for breakfast, as a snack, or as a dessert. It is a real novelty, lots of fun, and versatile for family or guests. I received this recipe from Mari, another Finn who lived near us when at graduate school. It's the best I've found.

- 3 Eggs
- 3 cups Milk, fresh or "soured"
- 1 ½ cups Flour
- ¾ cups Sugar
- ¼ tsp Salt
- ½ cup Butter

Beat the eggs in a bowl or with your kitchen machine until fluffy. Add the sugar and beat some more. Now add the milk and flour that has salt in it, and continue beating.

In a large oven pan or cooking dish with rims at least 1-inch deep, melt the butter in a hot oven. Be ready to pull the pan from the oven as soon as the butter has melted. Pour the pancake mixture into the cooking pan or dish with the butter. Stir until the butter is very well mixed.

Bake at 425 F for 20-30 minutes. You can serve *Pannukakku* right out of the oven, with jam (especially strawberry jam), or fresh berries. And if you want to make it very festive, top it with some whipped cream.

    As a child in a household that had lost its home twice, I remember often hearing the remark: "What if another war comes?" Mother wouldn't throw away anything, especially if it had to do with foods that were scarce during and after the war. For better or worse, I carried this tradition into my own family trying to be economical during those years when our four children were young. Once I made a huge mistake. The children told me that the milk in their glasses was sour. I didn't believe them and insisted they drink it, promising them raisins if they did. After they finished with frowning faces, I decided to check it myself. They were right. Even though I apologized, the kids took every chance to tease me about this over the passing years. Even now, every time they offer "pannukakku" to their friends, they don't spare me from this story.

    As the Pannukakku bakes, it is amusing to watch how the batter starts to bubble up. Sometimes it rises, and the bubbles stay, and sometimes they don't. You will see what I mean. There is a Finnish saying: "*Everything turned out like Pannukakku.*" First it rose and looked promising and then it flattened out. Life is often like that. But with the oven pancake, whichever way it goes is fine. The taste is the same.

Pumpernickel Bread
from Raija's kitchen, Idaho

Servings: 2 loaves

This full-of-flavor Pumpernickel Bread recipe from my Finnish friend Raija helped us get though graduate school – a bestseller in my home bakery. It takes advantage of the healthy qualities of a rye bread as it brings you the nice spices of northern European bread and pastries.

Raija and her husband Keith

- 2 packages Yeast, active dry
- 1 ½ tsp Salt
- 3 ¼ cups Flour
- 2 cups Rye Flour
- 1 ¼ cups Water
- ½ cup Dark Brown Sugar
- 1 tsp Anise Seed
- 1 tsp Caraway Seeds
- 2 Tbs Butter
- 1/3 cup Molasses

In a small bowl soften the yeast in ½ cup warm water. Now, place the molasses, butter, seeds, salt and sugar into a large bowl. Add 1¼ cups boiling water and stir in until the butter is melted. Beat in 1 cup white flour until smooth. Cool to lukewarm. Stir softened yeast and water into this mixture, mixing well. Add rye flour and beat until stiff. Now, beat in enough of the remaining white flour to make a soft dough.

Turn onto a lightly floured surface, make a soft dough, and work the dough more with your hands if needed. Allow to rest 5-10 minutes. Then knead until the dough is smooth and does not stick to the surface. Form into a large ball, and put into a deep already greased bowl. Turn to bring the greased surface to the top. Cover with waxed paper and a towel.

Let your dough stand in a warm place until doubled in bulk (about 2 hours). Punch it down, and pull the edges to center. Turn the dough over completely in the bowl. You can now cover and let it rise again, about 1 ½ hours.

After your dough has risen, once again punch it down again and then turn it onto a lightly floured surface. Divide in half, into two round or oblong loaves. Place onto two greased 9-inch round pans (or put your loaves into 2 loaf pans) Cover and let rise until doubled (about 1 hour).

Bake at 350 F for 35-40 minutes. Brush the bread with milk once during the last 3 minutes of baking. Remove from pans to cool.

    We stopped by Keith's and Raija's Finlandia Ranch a few weeks after President Ronald Reagan had phoned to ask Keith to be the American ambassador to Finland. We were on leave from the embassy in Helsinki and traveling in a Volkswagen camper across the United States. We hoped the trip would give our four small children a better feel for the America they did not yet know well.

    The Finlandia Ranch was high in the Rocky Mountains, not far from the borders of Yellowstone National Park. From their cozy mountain ranch home they saw the majestic Teton Range across the southern horizon. And as Raija cooked and baked, she watched from her kitchen window as bear, moose, deer, and skunks wandered in front of the house and across the fields.

    Raija came as a Finnish bride to Keith's ranch in the early 1950's. It must have been a big contrast to what she was used to, but I have never known a happier couple than Raija and Keith. She brought together the best of Finland and America in her ranch home, both in its décor and her meals. The ranchers and farmers around them quickly gained an appreciation for her Finnish heritage as she learned theirs.

    We had been friends with Raija and Keith long before their appointment to Finland. It was just one of life's grand coincidences that we were to live and work in Helsinki together. My husband was from Idaho, and he and I had spent a year attending and teaching at a college there. I was a young, Finnish, and living in America for the first time. They were at our Idaho wedding on the banks of the beautiful Snake River.

    Raija gave me this bread recipe soon after we were married. A few years later, as I mentioned earlier, I started a home bakery to help pay the bills. This pumpernickel was a hit. I could sell as much of it as I had time to bake.

Walnut Bread
from Irma's kitchen, Italy

Servings: 2-3 loaves

This fantastic bread is from Irma's Umbrian Restaurant "La Mulinella" in Todi -- probably the best bread I had in Italy. I have spent a lot of time getting it into the right proportions, since the recipe she gave me made 10 or 20 loaves. It is a very tasty bread to accompany your dinner meal, to serve as an appetizer before the meal, or to toast and eat with a breakfast drink.

Irma

2 ¼ lb Flour

3 ½ scant tsp Yeast

1-2 tsp Sugar

2 cups warm Water

1 Tb (heaping) Salt

1 cup Extra Virgin Olive Oil

10 oz Walnuts, chopped

Add yeast to 1/3 cup of water (from the 2 cups). Then, stir in 1 or 2 teaspoons of sugar to help the yeast activate better. Stir well and set aside.

Pour the rest of the water and the oil (you might prefer slightly less oil, e.g., 2/3 cups oil, depending on your taste) and the salt into a large bowl and stir in some flour until mixed. Now add the activated yeast mixture to this mixture. Continue adding flour until you reach a nice consistency. Next, add your nuts and knead them well into your dough.

Cover the bowl with a clean cloth and let it rise until the dough is doubled. Divide it into 2 or 3 portions. Roll them into 2 long or 3 short rolls and set on a cookie sheet lined with the baking paper. I take 1-2 tablespoons olive oil and spread it with my fingers over the bread loaf.

Bake in a 350 F oven until done, 30-40 minutes depending on your oven. To serve, cut your Walnut Break into thin small slices.

Todi

This recipe is from Todi, an Etruscan hilltop town and one of the colorful cities in Italy's Umbria region. Umbria is a beautiful, verdant province not far from Rome and is sometimes called "il cuor verde d'Italia," (the green heart of Italy).

Our American friend Cathy lived in Umbria and recommended to us an enchanting (or possibly enchanted) country hotel that had a "new wing" (only 100 years old), an older wing (medieval), and a still older one (Roman – at least 1600 years old). We stayed in the medieval section, but enjoyed the library, in the ancient Roman tower. One of the hotel employees later told us that a ghost lived in the library, a woman dressed in black whom the owners and several guests had seen. We would have spent much less time in the library had we known earlier. But that's good advice anyway: most people go to Italy for its food, history, and color - not its libraries.

Cathy also recommended to us La Mulinella restaurant which she considered one of the best restaurants in Italy. No ghosts at La Mulinella, everything was just as we were told: an absolutely remarkable place to eat.

Irma, who owned and ran La Mulinella, was an older woman who in eight years had made it into a favorite Umbrian eating place that was so popular that there were even road signs directing us to its location. The eating area was small. Some of Irma's children and grandchildren helped serve.

The first thing I tried was this walnut bread that was served as we sat down. One bite overwhelmed me. After lunch, I wanted to walk straight into the kitchen to tell Irma what a wonderful bread she had created. Her granddaughter, our waitress, said it was one of the busiest times of the day, so I arranged to come back the next morning to meet Irma in her kitchen. She gave me the recipe, and now you have it.

American Chocolate Cake

Servings: 15

from Esther's kitchen, USA

This real American chocolate cake comes from a folk recipe handed down and enjoyed by many generations. I have served it everywhere.

Esther

Cake
2 cups All Purpose Flour

2 cups Sugar

4 Tbs Powdered Cocoa

½ cup Butter

½ cup Water

½ cup Buttermilk

1 tsp Cinnamon

1 tsp Baking Soda

2 large Eggs

1 tsp Vanilla extract

Icing
½ cup Butter

6 Tbs Milk

4 Tbs Powdered Cocoa

1 tsp Vanilla Extract

1 box Powdered Sugar (or enough to make a spreadable texture)

½ cup Nuts

Cake
Sift together the flour, cocoa, cinnamon, and sugar. Next, in a large sauce pan add the butter and water, heat to dissolve and then set aside. Now combine together the buttermilk, soda, vanilla, and eggs. (If you don't have buttermilk, you can use milk plus 2 tablespoons of vinegar.) Mix all three mixtures together well, and pour into a large (8 x 12 inch) greased and floured Pyrex dish. Bake 20 minutes at 400 F, until a toothpick inserted into the center comes out clean. *Ice the cake while it is still hot.*

Icing
Place the butter, milk, cocoa, and vanilla into a saucepan. Bring to a boil over low heat and remove from the heat. Add the powdered sugar. Beat well.

Spread the icing on the cake as soon as it is out of the oven. The icing will run across it nicely. If you wish, sprinkle with chopped nuts. (It takes 5 minutes to mix the icing, so you can time it to when the cake comes from the oven.)

Serve with vanilla ice cream.

    This is another family recipe that Esther, my husband's grandmother, taught me shortly after I first arrived in America. (See also her "Fried Chicken" recipe elsewhere in *The Nomad Chef*.) As a newlywed in a new country I often stood alongside Grandma in her farm kitchen, watching and learning while she cooked good American foods. In the tradition of the American countryside, Esther's and her husband Wayne's doors were always open, literally - never locked. And their table was always full of wholesome food welcoming any visitor who happened to stop by, expected or not.
    Whenever we ate at the tables of either of Mike's grandmothers, the dishes were perfect in their simplicity and refined tastes. These were folk kitchens at their best, developed through thousands of meals served to hard-working hungry people and from generations of experience.

The Nomad Chef

Baklava

Servings 15-20

from Herro's kitchen, Iraq

Herro, a young American diplomat, once made this delicious baklava for us from her Kurdish mother's recipe. Baklava is often thought of as a Greek sweet pastry dish, but it is found around the eastern Mediterranean, as are many other Greek dishes (which are not considered Greek when you find them in Turkey, Israel, or Lebanon.)

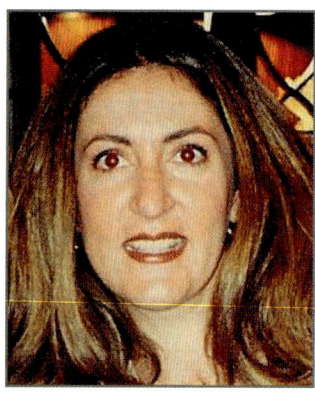

Herro

1 lb Fillo Pastry, sheets

4 cups Chopped Walnuts (14 ½ oz)

¼ cup Sugar

1 tsp Cardamom

2 tsp Cinnamon

3 sticks Butter

Syrup mix
1 ½ cups Sugar

1 cup Water

2 Tbs Brandy (optional)

1 Tb Lemon Juice

1 tsp Vanilla

½ cup Honey

Grease the bottom of a deep Pyrex dish with butter. Make your filling by mixing the crushed walnuts with the sugar, cardamom and cinnamon. The walnuts should be ground to medium texture and slightly chunky. If I am using whole walnuts, I take a towel and pour half the amount of nuts on it and cover them with the other half of the towel. Then with a rolling pin I crush the walnuts into smaller pieces. The same for the remaining half. This works better for me than the food processor which leaves some of the pieces too finely ground.

I begin by opening the first fillo package and placing the filo strips on top of a towel. Now, cover them with another towel in order to prevent the filo from drying. You can also dampen the towel to better keep the filo from drying. Next, put 10 pieces of filo dough on the bottom of the pan, brushing each one with melted butter. Cover them with 1 cup of filling.

Now add another layer of 8 fillo leaves on top of the filling, brushing again each one with butter. Put another cup of filling on the top of these leaves. Repeat in the same manner two more times until you have used all the filling. Now add the remaining sheets of fillo on the top, again brushing after each leaf.

Take a sharp knife, cut the baklava into 1-inch wide diamonds or squares before you cook it. Sprinkle lightly with water so that the sides don't get too dry. If you have any butter left pour it over on the baklava so that it can soak between the cut slices. Bake at 355 degrees for 30 minutes or until golden.

Syrup
Mix the sugar, water and honey in a pan and let boil for about 20 minutes. Take the pan from the heat and add lemon, and vanilla. Some people also add 2 Tbs brandy. When the baklava is done cooking, and while still hot, ladle the syrup over the top of the baklava slowly. Let it sit for 30 minutes

Herro came as a young girl to the United States with her parents who were Kurdish refugees from Iraq. I met her in Washington where we were both in the same Greek language class. It was easy for me to identify with Herro. When I was young, I, too, followed refugee parents and grandparents as they were driven from their home. We became good friends.

Later, at the American embassy in Athens, we saw each other often. One evening she joined a group of us embassy women at a concert by Greece's famous Greek-style crooner George Dalaras. Night life in Greece was late. Parties often started at 10:30, with dinner served at 11:00 or later. The same was true with concerts in the tavernas and restaurants in the Plaka district, situated at the foot of the Acropolis. The Dalaras concert started at 11:00 pm. But in Athens, do as the Athenians do, and that is what we did, enjoying a fun evening and warm atmosphere. People start emerging from tavernas and restaurants about 1:00 am or later, and the city is as lively as at noon. It was a good break from the heavy workload many carried, and the constant terrorist threat that our embassy people faced then.

Herro became an outstanding American diplomat, later assigned as an advisor to the American Vice President. She worked hard and was a great example of the American dream. But she didn't forget her traditions. And this Baklava is one of them.

Greek crooner Dalaras with Herro, Consul General Betsy Anderson and myself during a late night concert in millennia-old Plaka at the foot of the Acropolis

Buttermilk Cake
from Kaija's kitchen, Finland

Serves: 15

This Finnish dry cake from Kaija's recipe superbly blends a number of spices to set it apart from any dry cake you have tasted before.

Kaija and her husband Matti

- 1 ½ cups Buttermilk
- 2 tsp Baking Soda
- ½ cup dark Syrup
- ½ cup Sugar
- 1 cube Butter
- 1 tsp Cloves, ground
- 1 tsp Cinnamon
- 1 tsp Ginger
- 1 tsp Cardamom, ground
- ½ tsp Orange Peel
- 1 cup Raisins
- 1 cup Dried Apples, cut small
- 1 ½ cups Flour

Mix the buttermilk (you can also use plain or berry flavored yogurt), soda, and sugar. Combine the syrup and melted butter and let them cool slightly before adding to the buttermilk mixture.

Mix separately the spices, raisins and dried apples (or other kind of dried fruit) with the flour. Then add it to the previous mixture. The raisins and dried fruit make the cake moist. The taste of the cake improves when it gets older.

Bake in a cake pan that has been greased and dusted well with flour or with bread crumbs on the lower rack of the oven at 350 F, for about 1 hour. Test with a toothpick for the doneness. Remove the cake from the pan when it has cooled completely.

Note: Instead of flour, you can also use finely grated coconut or almonds to dust the cake pan.

"Your friends are my friends and my friends are your friends," so goes the verse. That's how it was with Kaija, who gave me this excellent dry cake recipe. She, her husband Matti, and I were friends when we were young. Later, when I moved to live in the US, Kaija and Matti "adopted" my parents. This was important for all of us. Being an only child, my move from Finland was especially painful. Kaija's parents were both gone. It made life so much easier for me to know that Kaija and Matti were near my family. And I think their friendship with my parents grew to be independent of me. That was a beautiful thing.

My parents, like the rest of the Finns, drank coffee like water. They started their day's work with a pot of hot coffee, they filled their thermoses with coffee to drink at work, and the very first thing they did when they arrived home was to put a kettle on the stove before starting evening chores.

Maybe this is the reason why the "coffee table" has been so important in Finnish tradition. People often offer friends more than one type of dry cake with their coffee when they visit. A buttermilk cake like Kaija's one has probably stood beside a date cake (see the recipe elsewhere) or another sugar cake millions of times on Finnish coffee tables. This recipe that Kaija shared with me is a particularly good one that you are sure to enjoy.

Chocolate Mousse Pie

from Katerina's kitchen, Greece

Servings: 8-10

Katerina made this pie several times a week for the coffee shop at the Golden Fox Hotel on the Greek island of Corfu. It is a sweet temptation next to a soft drink or something warm to drink in the afternoon, and definitely is a nice farewell to a lovely dinner.

Katerina and her Chocolate Mousse Pie

2 tsp Honey

2 tsp Cointreau (optional)

1 ½ cups Cream

1 lb Chocolate, dark

3 - 4 oz. Almonds

White Cake Bottom

Crush the almonds. Place your ready cake bottom in a 9-10 inch cake or pie pan. Now cover the cake with the crushed almonds. In a separate dish, break or crush the chocolate into small pieces. Mix the honey, liqueur, and chocolate together. Warm your cream to the boiling point in a sauce pan. Now you can add the warm cream to the chocolate mixture and stir well. Pour the hot chocolate mixture over the cake bottom. Refrigerate until hard.

P.S. If you wish, you can grate orange peeling from 1 orange into the chocolate mixture before pouring it onto the cake bottom.

This was our breakfast when we were in Corfu one year on Easter. It probably is not the healthiest way to start your day, but if you stay up late celebrating Greek Easter traditions and need energy the next morning, this cake will give it to you is a most exquisite way.

The recipe is from Katerina. Her family owned and operated The Golden Fox hotel and restaurant that majestically overlooked Corfu's beautiful Paleokastritsa (see my Crab Salad recipe for more about Katerina and her husband Nikos.) When we return to Corfu we always stay at the Golden Fox. Whenever we do so, Aleko, who now manages The Golden Fox, spoils us with hospitality.

We have been there twice on Greek Easter. Once, Aleko and his wife, Nina, took us Good Friday evening to celebrate at the village church. At 9:30 the Orthodox priests in their black robes proceeded according to custom through the church's centuries old wooden doors carrying the Epitafios, a flower-covered platform representing Christ's coffin. As we paraded behind, singers and the village band solemnly sang and played their way down the winding walkways, between dark ridges and village houses. The people whose families had lived there for hundreds of years warmly greeted each other in the candlelight Easter procession.

We remarked to Aleko that the villagers must know everything about everyone, friends and enemies. "If someone tells me he needs some bread, I'll give it to him," he answered. "But only stupid people make enemies." That was an impromptu Easter message! And what tradition, anchoring their world against the drift of the aimless every day.

Aleko and Nina

Epitafios Procession

The Nomad Chef

Date Cake
Servings: 12

from Lempi's kitchen, Finland

I have served my mother's Date Cake to people everywhere on my nomadic adventures. They never cease to marvel at the richness and fullness of this unique coffee table cake.

Lempi

- ½ lb Dates, pitted and chopped
- 1 1/3 cup Water
- ½ lb Butter
- 1 tsp Baking Powder
- 1 1/3 cup Sugar
- 2 Medium Eggs
- 1 ½ cup All Purpose Flour
- 1 tsp Baking Soda
- 1 Tb Cocoa
- 1 tsp Vanilla

First, cover your dates with the water and bring to a boil. Cool.

Combine and cream together the sugar and butter. Now mix in the eggs, flour, cocoa, vanilla, baking powder, and baking soda. Stir into the date mixture.

Bake in a greased and floured loaf or ordinary cake pan at 350 F for about an hour until done.

    I know a lot of date cake recipes, but this one is dear to me because it's my mother's. Lempi was clever with her hands. As a young girl in Finland she studied hat design. She made hats and wore them as did so many women in that era. When Lempi was in her forties she developed a crippling form of rheumatoid arthritis and spent the last 25 years of her life in a wheel chair. During those years her view of the world was what she could see from her window. But she never lost an excitement for life and, writing with swollen fingers, she kept up a huge correspondence with her many friends.

    Lempi, whose name in Finnish means "love," was a splendid cook and homemaker, and would not let illness keep her from the kitchen. She loved parties, and in spite of her arthritis she was always planning occasions to have over friends and family. But as her paralysis progressed, she drafted my father Manne to work, and with her careful instruction he, too, became an outstanding cook in her kitchen. When friends were in their home, the coffee table was full of pastries and cakes like this one.

Finnish Cream Cake

Servings: 10-12

from Lempi's kitchen, Finland

This is a cake served for birthdays, any kind of celebration, or simply for the coffee table along with other pastries. You can be creative with the fillings and decorations. Let your imagination fly! You will like this cake so much that you will bake and serve it many times.

Cake
1 ½ cup Eggs (4-6 eggs)

1 ½ cup Sugar

1 ½ cup Flour

1 tsp Baking Powder

1 Tb Lemon Juice

1-2 Tbs Cornstarch or Potato Flour

Moistening Mixture
1-2 cups Fruit or Berry Juice

Filling
2 cups Berries

1 cup Heavy Whipping Cream

Some Sugar and Vanilla to sweeten the cream

Topping
1 additional cup of Berries to decorate the cake

Whipped Cream (sweetened)

Lempi and me

Cake Base

Beat the eggs until light and fluffy. Mix in the sugar and continue beating. Add the flour with the cornstarch or potato flour and fold carefully into the egg mixture. Pour into 2 well-buttered and floured 8-inch round cake pans or into 1 spring form cake pan. Bake in 350 – 375 F oven for 30 minutes or until the top springs back when touched lightly. Cool and remove from the pans. With a long knife, cut into layers. If you use 8-inch round pans, cut each layer horizontally into two layers. If you use a spring form pan, cut it into three layers.

Filling

Moisten each layer with the juice: place the first layer on a serving plate and moisten and fill with a layer of fruit and whipped cream. I mash the berries with a fork and stir in whipped cream. Raspberries or strawberries are perfect, and if I use strawberries I often mix with them one banana. You can also use berry jam if you don't have fresh berries available.

Cover with the second layer and repeat until the layers are stacked and filled. The cake can be stored in the refrigerator, and you can finish it later just before the eating time.

A perfect cake for any occasion: Easter...   *...Valentines...*

....Birthdays...   *...or whatever is on your calendar...*

Glaze (optional)
1 package Gelatin (unflavored)

1 cup Water

2 Tbs Sugar

1-2 cups Fruit Puree or Whipped Cream Whole Berries (sliced), or Fruit such as Grapes Bananas, Kiwi Fruit, etc.

Topping
Cover the top and sides of the cake with whipped cream and then decorate with berries (or if you don't have enough fresh berries take a bar of chocolate and grate it or sliver it onto the cake's top). As an alternative you can use a glaze (see below).

Glaze (optional)
Instead of covering the top with whipped cream, you can use a glaze. Soften the gelatin in ½ cup cold water. Heat the remaining ½ cup water and stir into gelatin mixture. Add the sugar. Chill the glaze until slightly thickened. Arrange the fruit or berries on the top and spoon the gelatin over the top giving a thin glaze. Frost the sides of the cake with the fruit puree or with the whipped cream. Chill.

They had very little when Lempi and her parents arrived as refugees in central Finland at the end of World War II. My father was missing in action and, unknown to Lempi, he was a prisoner of war in the Soviet Union. Mother had a few photographs she had carried with her. This one has a hole from the tack that held it to the wall while she refused to believe her husband was dead.

Though they had lost so much, they still carried with them a set of proud Karelian traditions that included what you served guests when they came to visit. Mother had recipes like this one for many different cakes and pastries.

I remember when my father, Manne, finally arrived home from the prison camp. He weighed only 100 pounds, but he was fortunate to be alive. Mother fed him continually, and probably a cream cake like this one was on the table often as she brought her starved husband back to health.

Every summer when strawberry season came she made this cake for the weekend, whether hosting a party or not. It was a must and looked lovely on our summer table.

Frozen Berry Dessert

from Ulla's kitchen, Finland

Servings: 6

This recipe is "Life in a Bowl": sweet and sour, hot and cold. Simple, but grand enough to serve to a movie star.

Ulla

- 1 cup Cream
- 1 cup Brown Sugar
- 6 cups frozen Berries

Combine cream and sugar together in a saucepan. Carefully bring to a boil and then reduce heat, stirring the entire time until the sauce begins to thicken. Be careful not to let it cook so long that it becomes hard.

Pour hot over dessert bowls full of frozen tart berries, such as black currants, red currants, or cranberries. (Cranberries work better in combination with something less tart, such as blackberries.) Serve while the berries are still frozen and the sauce is still steaming. The sauce will thicken as it cools.

    This delightful life in a bowl recipe is from Ulla, whose salmon recipe is also in *The Nomad Chef*. It takes advantage of the richness of Finnish cuisine to blend the best of nature into a dish that tickles your taste buds from beginning to end.

    I served Frozen Berry Dessert at the end of a luncheon I organized in honor of Daniel Day-Lewis. Daniel was in Athens for the opening of his movie, "Gangs of New York." He had generously agreed with the studio to donate proceeds from the showing to the Greek cerebral palsy organization.

    I told my husband, Michael, that I planned to greet Daniel's arrival by joking with a famous line from one of his movies which started with him saying: "Take off your clothes." Michael's reaction was very negative, as I expected, and I agreed not to use the line.

    After the luncheon, however, I couldn't resist. As Daniel was getting ready to leave, I said, "I was going to greet you with your line, 'Take off your clothes,' but Michael wouldn't let me." Daniel, with his piercing eyes, looked at me and erupted with a hearty laugh. "If I'd had a few glasses of wine, I would have," he replied. Michael survived, as I also expected.

Genoise Gateau

Servings: 12

from Ian's kitchen, Italy

This splendid Genoise Gateau is Ian's recipe Named after Genoa, Italy, it belongs to a family of light and airy sponge cakes. This recipe produces an impressive presentation especially if you cut and mold the chocolate sides the way he did. Whether that way, or done simply by frosting, it is a cake you won't forget.

Ian

Cake Base:
1 cup Sugar

8 Eggs

1 ¾ cups Flour

¼ cup clarified Butter

Ganache Filling
2/3 cup Butter

12 oz. Chocolate Bar (dark)

1 tsp Vanilla

1 Tb Sugar

2/3 cup Heavy Cream

For Moistening Gateau
3/4 cup Orange Juice

Genoise Cake Base

Pre-heat your oven to 375 F. Place the sugar and eggs in a Bain-marie (or in a "water bath" or double boiler) and heat, whisking all the while until the mixture reaches about 80 F. Warming the eggs and sugar this way helps melt the sugar so that the eggs will reach their full volume when beaten.   Remove from the bowl and beat for 20 minutes, until it has a ribbon consistency. The batter starts out yellow but will become lighter and paler until it reaches a cream color as it thickens.

Fold in the flour gently. Do not over work it. Fold in the warmed clarified butter. (The difference between a regular sponge cake and a Genoise is that adding warm clarified butter makes the Genoise light and tender with a nice flavor. The butter needs to be warm so it does not solidify once it is added to the cake batter, causing streaks, or worse, causing the batter to deflate.)

Pour into an 8 or 9-inch cake pan that has been buttered and floured Cook about 30 minutes, or until ready. When done, place on a cooling rack. Cool completely.

Ganache Filling

Place all the ingredients into a pan and heat in a Baine-marie (or in a

- 1 Tb Grand Marnier, or Rum (optional)

Topping:
- 1 pint Berries (or Cherries)

- 10 oz. Chocolate bar (optional)

Raspberry Sauce

- 1 pint fresh Raspberries

- ¼ cup Sugar

- 1 Tb Lemon Juice

double boiler). Then cool to room temperature.

Gateau

Slice the cake base into three layers. Then, seal the bottom of the cake with a light layer of Ganache and cool. Now, using a basting brush or spoon, moisten each layer with the juice. Some people add a tablespoon Grand Marnier or rum to the orange juice. The sealed bottom will keep the juice inside the cake. Next, cover each inside layer with a thick filling of Ganache, leaving enough Ganache to frost the sides, if you decide to go in this direction (see below). Set each layer on top of each other.

Decorating - Sides

There are two ways to cover the sides. The first is simply to use your left over Ganache to frost the sides, as you would with any cake. Should you decide to decorate in this way, you may need to prepare a larger amount of Ganache, perhaps multiplying the above Ganache measurements by 1 ½ times.

Ian, however, took a more dramatic approach by molding strips of chocolate around the cake. (See the photos) You do this by first measuring with paper the circumference of the cake to size the chocolate strip you will need. Next, melt the 10 oz chocolate bars in the Bain-marie or double boiler, and then spread the melted chocolate onto waxed paper in the size and shape you measured with the paper. (You can place the measured strip of paper underneath the wax paper to guide you.) You may find it is easier to work with two strips each half the length. Put into the freezer until the chocolate is hard, but still moldable. Carefully remove the chocolate from the waxed paper, and mold the strip (or two strips) around the cake. Place in the refrigerator to cool.

Decorating - Top

Raspberry Sauce - In a saucepan cook for 5-10 minutes the raspberry sauce berries and sugar until the berries are broken. Then add the lemon juice and cool.

Topping: Just before eating, layer the top of the cake with 1 pint whole berries, and cover with the raspberry sauce. You can use mixed berries, raspberries, or even cherries.

Cut a strip of paper the size you need to fit around your cake and place beneath wax paper

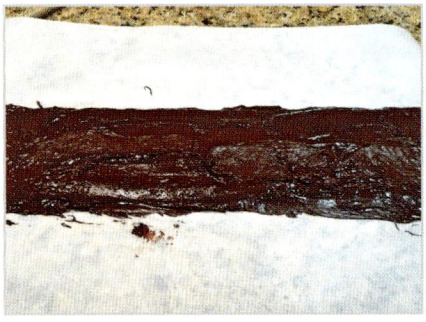

Spread melted chocolate over the wax paper in the shape of your pattern

One beautiful Easter week our daughter Kristiina's family was visiting us in Rome. It was their young daughter's and our oldest granddaughter Karelia's first trip to Rome, and it was her birthday. What a surprise it was when after our birthday party dinner, Ian emerged from the kitchen with a Genoise Gateau birthday cakes. Our eyes looked at Ian and then dropped to what he had in his hands. The cake was beautiful, and so was the moment. (You will learn more about Ian from other of his recipes in *The Nomad Chef*.)

Mamsel's Torta

from Kaija's kitchen, Finland

Servings 10-12

Just about everyone likes cakes. If you don't like to eat them, without any doubt you like to look at them. They are a visual pleasure. Especially, if you like meringue, Kaija's Mamsel's Torta is one of the best cakes you ever find . Kaija's family lovingly calls her cake pahvikakku which, in Finnish means "cardboard cake," referring to its meringue layers. Her pahvikakku has been a great hit in their family. Whenever there is an important family get together this delightful cake is must on the festive table. And so it has been on ours. When we have company and I prepare this delicacy someone eventually says, "Oh, do you mind… if I take the last piece?"

Kaija

<u>3 Meringue Bottoms</u>
You will need 3 meringue bottoms, each made with:

4 Egg Whites

2/3 cup Powdered Sugar

3 ½ oz Toasted Almonds or Hazelnuts, ground

<u>Filling for the entire Torta</u>

½ cup Sugar

½ cup Water

4 Egg Yolks

2 cubes Butter, (1 cup)

1 ½ oz Baking Chocolate

7 oz Whipping Cream

1 tsp Vanilla Sugar, optional

Meringues

Whip the 4 egg whites stiff. (The eggs need to be at room temperature.) Stir in sifted powdered sugar. Draw an 11-inch circle on parchment paper, and then grease and cover the paper with ground nuts. Spread the meringue onto your circle. Sprinkle carefully more ground nuts on the top.

Bake in a low oven temperature of 250 F for 2 hours, or until it is dry and firm. Switch the oven off and leave the meringue in the oven for a half an hour with the door partially open.

Now repeat this process to bake the other two meringue bottoms. You can make these meringue bottoms earlier and wrap them well with clear wrap to keep them crispy.

Filling

Make the filling when you are nearly ready to serve the cake. Boil the water and sugar into a syrupy type liquid. You have to cook it long enough for it to get pasty. To check it, pour a spoonful into a cup of cold water. If it holds together like a soft ball, it's ready (approx. 20 minutes). Whip the egg yolks a little, and then pour the hot mixture over the egg yolks, whipping strongly. Now, pour the mixture back

into the original hot cooking pan and continue to whip until the mixture has cooled off completely. I put my pan in a larger dish that contains ice cubes in it to help to cooling process.

Now add the melted chocolate and vanilla sugar. (**Note**: The optional vanilla sugar is sometimes difficult to find. I have bought it at "Penzeys Spices.") At the end, add the 1 cup of butter little by little. Whip until the mixture is smooth and foamy.

Assembly

Assemble the cake by placing one meringue bottom on a platter. Spread half of the filling on top this first bottom. Whip the cream and spread about one third of it over the bottom. Now add the second meringue layer and cover it with filling and cream in the same method. Add the top layer.

It is best not to assemble your cake until just a few hours before serving if you prefer a crunchy taste. You can always make the filling in advance. But if you prefer moist cake it is best to assemble your cake two days or so before serving so that the cake has time to moisten completely through.

P.S. If one of your meringues has a yellowy, sugary texture, you can still use it. Just place it upside down on the bottom.

Kaija was a home economics teacher, talented and gifted with many skills. You could give her a sheep and from the sheep she would prepare an outfit to wear. Kaija could shear the sheep, spin the wool on a spinning wheel into yarn, weave the yarn on a loom into fabric, and finally, make an outfit from the fabric. Where can you find someone like that today?

"I have been blessed with working hands," Kaija once told me. Yes, blessed hands and an ability to work hard. As just a young girl in impoverished post-war Finland, her father sent her and her sister to the city to learn their own way through life. They found a room to rent, earned their own money, and educated themselves.

Kaija became the wife of the owner of a successful cleaning products firm, the proud mother of three exceptional children, and grandmother to their beautiful families. When her husband, Anssi, passed away, the children took over the business. Kaija was in her seventies, but didn't lose a step. We once visited her Helsinki home to find her in the yard laying a pathway of concrete squares. She pulled off her gloves, and served us something exquisite to eat, including Mamsel's Torta.

And by the way, Kaija always served two different desserts to finish a meal, just to be sure no one left weighing less than they arrived. (But Kaija had no problem with her weight - she was cross country skiing in the winter and swimming in the summer well into her seventies.)

*Helsinki's South Harbor,
around which stands a delightful outdoor market*

Oatmeal Cake
from Joanne's kitchen, Idaho

Servings: 12-16

Everyone loves this delicious oatmeal sheet cake. It is vintage folk kitchen with all the simplicity and richness that comes from the best handed down recipes.

Joanne

Cake
1 ½ cups boiling Water

1 cup Quick Oats

½ cup Shortening

½ cup Butter

1 cup Sugar

1 cup Brown Sugar, packed

1 ½ cup Flour

2 Eggs

1 tsp Cinnamon

¾ tsp Nutmeg

½ tsp Salt

1 tsp Baking Soda

Topping
4 Tbs Butter, melted

1 cup Nuts, chopped

½ cup Brown sugar, packed

¼ cup Canned Milk

1 cup Coconut

Cake
Pour hot water over the shortening and butter, and stir until they are melted. Now, add the oatmeal and stir well. Mix separately all the remaining ingredients together. Blend the oatmeal mixture with the second mixture. Bake at 350 F in a 9 x 13 inch pan for 30 minutes.

Topping
Combine and mix together all the topping ingredients. Then, put your topping mixture on top the cake after it is baked, but still warm. Place the cake back into the oven and broil for about 5 minutes or until browned.

    Joanne was born and raised in Nampa, Idaho, "a real city girl," she called herself. In the summer she and her two sisters spent time on her great uncle's and aunt's Idaho ranch, riding horses, and chasing pigs. The house had no indoor plumbing, and they got water from a big barrel near the front door. Her uncle Bill milked 100 cows twice a day, and fed them hay from a horse-drawn wagon. Every time they visited the ranch, Aunt Bertha made her Oatmeal Cake in a cook stove heated with wood. Joanne told me that this recipe had been in the family at least for decades. "Aunt Bertha passed away in the early 1980's," she told me, "but her recipe lives on."

Joanne's husband Fred

We met Joanne and her husband, Fred, when we moved to the majestic Buckskin Canyon above Pocatello, Idaho. They were our next-door neighbors. In the Idaho canyons, "next-door" doesn't crowd anyone too much. We admiringly called Fred and Joanne and our other neighbors "mountain people." They knew about this sometimes rough life, from how to deal with moose, bear, and mountain lions, to how to keep your steep driveway clear during the snowfalls that reached up to 25 feet by winter's end. Living in the canyon for its beauty and isolation, they were not on your doorstep twice a day. But they were there when you needed support, such as Joanne's sweet gesture of bringing her oatmeal cake to the home of Mike's mother, whom she had never met, when his father passed away.

We had Fred, Joanne, and Dick, another neighbor who had recently lost his wife, over for Greek meals and they had us in the summer for cook-outs in their back yard. One July evening when we were at Fred's and Joanne's, a huge bull moose, nearly six-foot tall at the shoulder, wandered from the woods to the other side of the yard and sat down. He didn't bother us, and we didn't bother him during our pleasant dinner and conversation.

While eating at Joanne's and Fred's house a moose joined us for dinner

*Joanne's and Fred's home was through the trees.
Nature was the neighborhood*

Pavlova

from Nellie's kitchen, South Africa

Servings: 20

This luscious recipe is from my South African neighbor, Nellie. It requires a little bit of work, but it's perfect for when you want to make a big impression. I have used this Pavlova often for representational occasions. (See also Nellie's "Tenderloin" recipe)

Meringue
12 extra large Egg Whites (at room temperature)

2 ½ cups Granulated Sugar

1/8 cup Vanilla Extract

1/8 cup Vinegar

1/4 cup Corn Flour (or maybe just a little less)

a pinch of Salt

Crème Patisserie Filling
6 Egg Yolks

1/3 cup All Purpose Flour

¼ cup Sugar

3 cups warm Milk

1 tsp Vanilla Extract

1 Tb Butter

1/4 cup Whipping Cream

Chantilly Cream
2 ½ cups Cream

4 Tbs Sugar

2 tsp Vanilla Extract

¼ cup Whiskey (optional)

¼ cup Honey

Nellie

Pavlova
Line two cookie sheets with wax paper or baking paper. (If you butter the sheets, allow the butter to set for a few minutes before flouring lightly.) In a spotless dry glass bowl, beat eggs whites until stiff, but not dry. Mix in 1 tsp of your sugar with each egg white as you add it, and beat for a few seconds. This will give body and a glossy sheen.

Gradually fold the remaining sugar into the mixture together with the vanilla extract, vinegar, and corn flour, and beat until whites form stiff glassy peaks. Using a spatula, spread the mixture into two 8-9 inch rounds of equal size, one each on a separate cookie sheet.)

Bake for 1 ½ hours at 300 F using only bottom heat. Open the oven door and allow the Pavlova to dry out for a further 25-30 minutes. Cool and place the Pavlova carefully on a platter. (**Note**: If you are making the meringue a few days before assembling the Pavlova, store it in a closed container, since the meringue sheets pull moisture from the air and lose their crispness.)

Crème Patisserie
To prepare the crème patisserie, whisk together all the ingredients, *except* for the butter and cream, in an enamel saucepan over low heat until the mixture is thick enough to coat a wooden spoon and it

just comes to a boil. (The flour will prevent it from curdling.) Remove, add the butter, and whisk somewhat longer. When completely cool, fold in ¼ cup thick cream for an extra silk finish.

Chantilly Cream
To prepare the chantilly cream, chill the cream thoroughly. Pour into a chilled bowl. Whip until it begins to thicken, and add sugar, vanilla extract, whiskey and honey. Continue beating until it holds its shape on the beaters.

Assembly
Spread the first Pavlova layer with crème patisserie. Put on the second meringue and cover it with chantilly cream. Decorate with fresh fruits, chipped butter-brickle (Heath or Dajm bars), or slivered chocolate.

Pavlova dessert was invented in commemoration of a visit by the great Russian Ballerina, Anna Pavlova, to New Zealand and Australia. There is a dispute between the two countries over which of them gets the honor of being the true home of the recipe. I'm not sure that South Africa has joined the quarrel, but it was my lovely South African friend Nellie, our neighbor in Pretoria, who gave me this version that she used in her catering business. The dishes Nellie made fit any gourmet. She was one of the best cooks ever, and this is one of her best desserts.

Nellie was a schoolteacher by profession, but was also a talented interior designer. Her large thatched roofed home was a knockout in color, furnishings, and taste. At 4:00 sharp each afternoon Nellie fed the birds on the patio behind her home. Starting at 3:45, hundreds of wild birds, some of which may have migrated from as far away as Siberia, would begin crowding the power lines overhead waiting for Nellie to arrive. When Nellie and her husband, Hermann, moved away, I inherited the birds. I got to know them, and I found that they knew us well, too. From 3:45 until feeding time they were out there peering from their perches into my kitchen, reacting to any sudden movements inside the house, and waiting for me to emerge with their afternoon treat. At 4:15 the food was gone, and so were the birds.

Profiteroles
from Peter's kitchen, Greece

Servings: 6

Small cream-filled puff pastry balls covered with good chocolate, profiteroles are lots of fun and far from the ordinary dessert. You can serve them on a flat platter heaped under a dark chocolate sauce. And please note how your guests can't stop devouring them.

Peter

Pastry
1 cup Water

½ cup Butter

1 cup Flour, sifted

5 Eggs room temperature

Filling
2 large boxes Instant Vanilla Pudding Mix

4 ½ cups cold Milk

1 pint Whipping Cream

Balls
Melt the butter with water in a saucepan. Remove from the heat. Beat the flour quickly and forcefully into the mixture and then return to the heat. With a wooden spatula or spoon, stir the mixture for another minute or two, until the sides come clean.

Remove from the heat once again and pour into a clean bowl. Stir for a short while to cool slightly. Now, add the egg mixture little by little. You will want your pastry to hold its shape. The mixture should be a little stiff so that it can go through a food decorator.

Fill a food decorator with the dough using a large tip, and pour about 30 pieces onto a greased baking dish, about 1 ½ inches wide, each. Bake at 400 F for 10 minutes, then 375 F for 10 minutes, and then leave in a 100 F oven for ½ hour. Do not remove them from the oven until they are quite firm to the touch. Cool the shells away from any draft before filling.

Filling
Add cold milk to the pudding mixes and stir until they thicken. Fold in the whipped cream (without sugar). Now you can cut the puffs three-quarter the way through horizontally with a sharp knife. If there are any damp dough filaments inside, be sure to remove them. Open each puff and fill with your filling. Pile them on a large platter into a

mound. Dribble Peter's Chocolate Sauce (see below for the recipe) over the piled profiteroles.

Optional: sprinkle with icing sugar through a sifter, and add toasted almonds.

Variations
You can also fill the puffs with softened vanilla ice-cream and cover with the chocolate sauce. Filled puffs which have been dipped in the chocolate sauce can also be served with a strawberry sauce.

  There are not too many Italian desserts, but this one is spectacular, and Peter, who gave me the recipe, was a master at making them. Everyone is fond of profiteroles. They are colorful and eye catching. I will never forget the sight when we attended a large party in Milano and found on the dessert table a mountain of these delicious chocolate balls.
  It is said that Caterina de' Medici, who married French king Henry II, introduced France to profiteroles from her home in Florence. Caterina was the daughter of the magnificent Lorenzo Medici family. At the time, Renaissance Florence was the center of civilized splendor. That pretty much describes this dessert. If you want civilization, this is your recipe! Profiteroles are literally fit for a king (and film directors).

Ponte Vecchio in Florence

Perfect Chocolate Sauce
from Peter's kitchen, Greece

If you are a chocoholic like I am, the difference between a good and poor chocolate sauce is the difference between living and eking out an existence. This chocolate sauce is from Peter, my Greek chef and mentor, and is just full of rich living. It is a perfect chocolate sauce to top a grand mound of profiteroles. But you will have no problem imagining many other uses for it.

Peter

7-8 oz. Dark Chocolate

1 can (12 oz.) Evaporated Milk

¼ cup Gran Marnier, or 2 Tbs Almond Extract

2 Tbs Butter (optional)

Melt the chocolate in a double boiler. Remove from heat and add butter. Then stir in the milk and Gran Marnier or almond extract. And you are ready to go with a sinful chocolate topping for profiterole, ice cream, or other dessert!

Never on Sunday" director Jules Dassin and "Love Story" director Arthur Hiller reminiscing after dinner in our home in Athens

    I served Peter's profiteroles with this elegant chocolate sauce one evening at a dinner in honor of Arthur Hiller, the director of the movie *Love Story* and many more Hollywood productions. The dinner was a memorable and touching evening for everyone.

    The "drama" began at the dinner table. Jules Dassin was one of our other guests. He directed *Never on Sunday* and many others. By then in his mid-80's, Jules was one of those Americans blacklisted in Hollywood during the McCarthy years of the early 1950's.

    We loved the conversation and listened carefully as these two great directors exchanged stories. Towards the end of the dinner, just as Peter's profiteroles were being served, Jules turned to Arthur and said he had wanted to have his reputation restored in America. He added that he once even wrote to the president of the Directors Guild of America about it.

    Arthur put down his fork, looked a Jules, and then said he was the guild president who received that letter. Arthur continued that the guild had agreed to Dassin's request several years before to reinstate him in good standing.

    Deeply moved, Jules sat quietly and then said somehow he had never received the guild's response. He was overwhelmed. A poignant silence surrounded the table. Jules' eyes were filled with tears. We were all astonished to unexpectedly experience a profound moment between two film industry giants.

Rhubarb & Strawberry Dessert Soup
from my family's kitchen, Finland Servings: 4-6

This versatile family recipe makes a popular Scandinavian dessert soup that can be served in several delicious ways. It is nice to eat as a dessert topped with whipped cream. Or, you can pour it over vanilla ice-cream. It is also very good for breakfast over rice pudding or cream of wheat. In Finland we often have a bowl of this soup with cinnamon rolls or alongside "Pulla" sweet bread (recipes for both are found elsewhere in The Nomad Chef).

4 cups Rhubarb

1/2 - 1 cup Sugar, depending on how sweet you like it

6- 10 oz bag Frozen Strawberries

1 Stick Cinnamon, optional

3-6 Tbs cold Water depending how thick or runny you want the soup

3-6 Tbs Cornstarch or Potato Flour, as above

Cut the rhubarb into 1-inch pieces. Bring 4 cups water to a boil in a saucepan and add the cut rhubarb, sugar and cinnamon. Cook the rhubarb mixture until the pieces break down into strings. Keep an eye on the cinnamon stick, as soon as it starts to break, discard it. This will happen before the rhubarb is done.

In a large mug or bowl, mix 3 - 6 tablespoons water and the cornstarch very well until it is a fine paste without any lumps. Lift the rhubarb pan from the heat for a moment and with a wire whisk mix in the water-cornstarch mixture. Return the pan back to the stove again and, stirring with a wooden spoon the entire time, bring the mixture to the boiling stage. Immediately remove it from the hot stove.

Now pour your sack of frozen strawberries into the rhubarb mixture. This cools off the hot soup nicely. Check the sweetness and add a little extra sugar if your taste requires. Pour the soup into a nice serving bowl and sprinkle just a little bit of sugar on the top to prevent a film from forming.

Serve topped with whipped cream, or alternatively you can pour the soup over a scoop of vanilla ice cream.

If you don't have strawberries you can prepare the soup as it is with just the rhubarb, but I personally prefer it with the strawberries. You can also make the soup from frozen rhubarb. You might have to adjust the cornstarch-water mixture depending how much water the rhubarb contains.

    Rhubarb when prepared properly can be one of the most flavorful of all garden vegetables, and nutritious, as well. This was my childhood, growing up with the smell of fresh rhubarb soup cooking in the kitchen.

    One of the many things you looked forward to after the long winters was the pleasures of rhubarb and strawberries. It was a time when many foods and ingredients were scarce. But rhubarb was inexpensive and an easy vegetable to grow at the back of the garden close to the compost hill. Our rhubarb leaves were as large as children's umbrellas. We used to play games with the leaves using all kinds of imagination.

Supreme au Chocolat
from Paulette's kitchen, Italy

Servings: 12 – 15

Everyone loves this mousse, which is simply the best I have ever had in any country from any chef. Of all my recipes, this one that continues to raise most the eyebrows of everyone who tastes it.

Paulette

16 oz. Semi-sweet Chocolate

1½ tsp Almond Extract

2 Tbs Amaretto (optional)

10-12 Eggs

1 cup Whipping Cream

   Grated Chocolate

   Maraschino Cherries, or Slivered Almonds

Note: You can use milk chocolate in place of semi-sweet, but the result will be different. Try them both. See which you like best. I go with the darker mousse.

Melt the chocolate in a double boiler well so that it isn't lumpy, but doesn't burn. You will need to separate the egg yolks from the whites, keeping the egg whites for later. (Make sure not to get any yolk into the whites, and if you do, you must get it out before beating the whites later.) When the chocolate is melted in the saucepan, remove it from the heat and add one egg yolk at a time, stirring it in completely before adding the next. (This part is somewhat laborious. If I'm doing it alone, I have 10-12 small glasses or cups ready with the individual egg yolks, and one bowl full of the egg whites.) The mixture gets harder to stir with each egg yolk, for the first 6-8 yolks. I often do this together with my handy husband, Michael, to help.

When the yolks are mixed carefully into the chocolate, beat the egg whites until stiff. Then add the egg whites one spoonful at a time, folding them carefully into the chocolate mixture. Always stir clockwise and slowly so as not to lose the whipped egg whites' texture. You can avoid getting lumps by stirring deep to make sure all the chocolate on the bottom and sides ends up mixed smoothly with the egg whites. When completed, mix in the almond extract or Amaretto.

Pour the mixture into a nice serving dish, or divide it into small individual dishes (or wine glasses) and chill in the refrigerator for at least two hours. Whip cream with sugar and vanilla. Cover the hardened mousse completely with a thick layer of the cream. Decorate if you wish by adding slivered almonds, shaved chocolate slivers, or maraschino cherries on top the whipped cream.

Paulette (with our young daughter Kaarina) visited us in several places, including as in this photograph in Finland, and was like an auntie to our children. She had many wonderful recipes from her years living around the Mediterranean.

Our friend Paulette gave me this recipe when my husband was still a green diplomat and I was a young (-er) wife and mother. Paulette lived in Italy, but was Egyptian. Raised in Cairo with servants and a French nanny, she was quatra-lingual in Arabic, French, Italian, and English. Paulette had lived in many countries around the Mediterranean working for an American multinational company. She was older, never married, and a great friend and auntie to us. With our small children, we became her extended family, and our friendship continued throughout the years.

Our road through life has always had many intersections where we meet again friends we have known at other times and places, and this was true in the case of Paulette, too. We met up with her once on the north rim of the Grand Canyon. She was traveling with friends, and we were winding our way across the United States in a Volkswagen camper while on leave from our post in Europe. The idea behind our trip was to make sure that our children, who had British teachers at school, learned as much about Thomas Jefferson and Crazy Horse as they knew about Guy Fawkes.

Another time, Paulette visited us in Finland. She woke up early in the mornings, as if she were in Cairo again surrounded by all her servants. "Where is my breakfast?" she commanded. I just smiled and showed her where to find it. Yes, Paulette was one of those truly lovable characters you meet especially in the Mediterranean countries, totally colorful and authentic.

Whipped Cranberry Pudding

Servings: 4

from Selma's kitchen, Finland

Whipped Cranberry Pudding, or "Air Pudding," as it is called in Finland, is a simple, homey, healthy dish that both children and adults like. Rich in iron, vitamin C, and calcium, it can be used as a breakfast porridge or as a dessert.

Selma

4 cups Cranberry Juice*

¾ cup Cream of Wheat (not instant)

¼ cup Sugar

*Instead of pure cranberry juice, I like to use a combination, such as cranberry-raspberry. You can also use fresh or frozen cranberries (1 lb cranberries and 5 cups water). Boil the cranberries in the water for about 15 minutes. Strain and sweeten the juice. Measure the juice and follow directions above.

Heat the juice. Whip in the Cream of Wheat, stirring quickly, and then cook until it thickens, about 2 ½ minutes.

Whip with your electric mixer or kitchen machine at the highest speed until light colored and fluffy, about 15- 20 minutes.

Serve with milk, cream, or whipped cream.

Note: I prefer uncooked Farina instead of Cream of Wheat, but it takes about 30 minutes to cook. I have also found that various farina flours work a little differently. You might want to experiment with which measurement - 2/3 cup or 3/4 cup of farina - works best with the farina you have.

    I remember how my grandmother Selma sat on a kitchen chair, the bowl between her knees, to whip unendingly our "Air Pudding" by hand. Fortunately, you will have your pudding with much less effort than that, but its many nutritious benefits will be just the same.

    We didn't have many varieties of food during the post-war years in Finland, and looking back I find it revealing that a delightful cuisine can develop even with meager ingredients. My family tried to be as economical as possible, but at the same time, they prepared many tasty dishes, such as this one. During the late summer and early fall, my parents went to the forest to pick wild lingon berries that are similar in taste and tartness to cranberries. They also gathered fresh blueberries, many mushroom varieties, and other berries from the floor of the forests that cover Finland. We ate some of these fresh, some we dried, and others, such as lingon berries, were stored for the winter in glass jars. This way we could have this nutritious dish and many others during the cold winter months.

Produce from supermarket shelves still cannot compete with nature's own when it comes to fresh berries and mushrooms picked straight from the forest floor